The World You Never See
Insect Life

The World You Never See
Insect Life

Theodore Rowland-Entwistle

In conjunction with Oxford Scientific Films Limited

Rand McNally & Company
Chicago · New York · San Francisco

Contents

Published in the United States by Rand McNally & Company, 1976
First published in the U.K. by The Hamlyn Publishing Group Limited
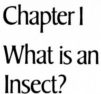 Designed and produced by
Intercontinental Book Productions
Copyright © 1976 Intercontinental Book Productions

ISBN: 0-528-81850-3
Library of Congress Catalog Card No. 76-8367

Colour Reproduction by Starf Photolito s.r.l., Rome, Italy
Printed in Italy

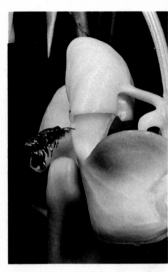

Foreword

The butterflies that flit through our gardens and the surrounding countryside are usually admired because of their bright and attractive colors, but few other insects receive such admiration or praise, and many are destroyed without a second thought or a second look. One can understand the swatting of mosquitos and other annoying flies, but even colorful beetles are trodden under foot without question, and the moths that come into our houses at night are, at best, unceremoniously thrown out of the window.

But these insects that intrude upon our lives, whether pleasantly or unpleasantly, are just a fraction of the huge world of insects. Most insects are simply not seen because they are so small or because they are so well camouflaged. Others are merely ignored. This unseen or unnoticed world of the insect is however, very interesting and also very important to mankind, but neither the interest nor the importance can be appreciated without a second look. In *The World You Never See*, Oxford Scientific Films give us that second look at many of the common insects around us, and also perhaps a first look at some of the more unusual insects. Through the many beautiful photographs in this book, we really *can* see something of the wonderful construction and behavior of the insects.

Oxford Scientific Films are uniquely qualified to produce this photographic study of the insect world, for they are professional zoologists who, although maintaining their links with the academic world, have turned their talents to filming of a very high quality. They are specialists in cinematography and, by combining their scientific expertise with an imaginative flair for communication and a remarkable talent for optical and mechanical engineering, they have created an organization which the London *Times* has described as 'the most technically advanced biological film unit in the world'. Although specializing in 'movies' — a great deal of their work has been seen on television and they have won numerous prizes in that medium — the company also does a lot of still photography for scientific purposes and for public consumption in books and magazines.

Specially designed studios and equipment are used, including optical benches and powerful yet heat-free lighting systems which enable very tiny insects to be photographed at very high magnifications while still going about their normal business. The ability to design and construct specialist equipment of this kind is one of OSF's outstanding features, and it has allowed their photographers to record on film numerous biological activities which had never previously been witnessed.

I am sure that looking at the brilliant photographs in this book will revolutionize the way in which many people look at insects. No longer will a butterfly be simply a pretty insect sitting on a flower: the observer will want to look for the coiled tongue with which the butterfly sucks nectar from that flower. This is not to say that there will be any lessening of the pleasure of looking at insects. On the contrary, there will be an enhancement of that pleasure when we know something of what makes the insects 'tick'. Even the humble housefly may well become an object of fascination when one realizes that it looks at us through about 4,000 lenses in each eye.

Oxford Scientific Films will, I am sure, open many eyes and stimulate them to look more closely at the world they have never seen.

Michael Chinery

Chapter I

What is an Insect?

Insects are probably the most familiar of all living creatures; they are the most numerous both in the number of different species and in the numbers of actual individuals. Around a million distinct species are known and probably there are at least as many more to be discovered. And for every one that you see there are hundreds all around that you do not, though they are close to you all the time. For insects are small, and they live in a hidden world of their own, a world whose secrets the camera is only just beginning to disclose.

It is possible to define an adult insect fairly precisely. It has a hard outer casing, nearly always three well-defined body sections and three pairs of legs. Most adult insects have wings and with few exceptions they are small creatures. Compared with mammals, they have their skeleton on the outside, and a nervous system that runs along the underside of their bodies, not along the back as in any vertebrate animal. Most importantly, an insect does not stay the same shape for the whole of its life; it goes through a process called metamorphosis. For example, a butterfly changes from egg to larva to pupa to adult.

Insect environments

Adapting over millions of years, insects have fitted themselves into almost every kind of habitat. You will find them in the hottest of tropical deserts and in the snow and ice of coastal Antarctica. They survive deep underground in caves, and thousands of feet up mountains. Only the sea has halted their advance, though some species of midge exist which prefer a submarine existence, and water striders have been found living on floating seaweed hundreds of miles from land. Also, a number of shore-dwelling insects spend most of their lives under the waves.

There are two major reasons why insects have become so successful. One is the incredible variety of food they eat. If a substance is even remotely edible, there is an insect to eat it. Some live on liquids like plant juices and the blood of other animals; some eat the humus or vegetable mold of soil. Insects exhibit a great range of specialized feeding habits. Leaves, fruits and stems of plants all have their particular beetles, bugs or caterpillars; fleas, lice and other parasites live on the bodies of larger animals and suck their blood.

1 Other insects thrive on the most unlikely sub-

2

stances, including peppermint, cigarettes and crude oil, while there are ptinid beetles that can live even in the corks of entomologists' killing jars.

Not all the creatures referred to as 'insects' or 'bugs' are in fact insects. Most of them, however, belong to one of the major divisions of the animal kingdom, the phylum Arthropoda. The arthropods form the biggest group of animals, and the insects form the largest part of the arthropods.

The arthropods derive their name from two Greek words which mean 'joint-footed,' although the arthropods are not so much joint-footed as joint-legged! The arthropods, unlike amphibians, reptiles, birds and mammals, have no internal skeleton. Instead they are covered by a horny casing, made largely of protein and a substance called chitin. The protein has come through a natural tanning process which makes it tough.

This outer casing takes the place of a skeleton, and is generally called an exoskeleton, or external skeleton. It serves exactly the same purpose as an internal skeleton, providing a frame for the body, and an anchoring point for muscles, but it also protects the body of the animal and keeps it from losing moisture.

Arthropods include a wide range of diverse animals. The phylum Arthropoda is divided into

1. The face of a fly, when seen in great detail, becomes an object of beauty and fascination. This hairy tachinid, covered in pollen from the flowers it has been visiting, comes from the United States and in its larval stage is parasitic on other insects.

2. The water louse *Asellus aquaticus* belongs to the crustacean order Isopoda, which also includes the woodlice. Crustacea differ from insects, having a greater number of limbs, which are branched. They also possess two pairs of antennae and unlike insects have no tracheal system for respiration.

3

4

3. This female centipede is coiled around her developing eggs and guarding them fiercely. One of her poison fangs is clearly visible. Although the fangs lie beneath the head, they are not associated with the mouthparts but are in fact modified front legs.

4. Spiders differ from insects, possessing four pairs of legs instead of three and having the body divided into only two parts. In this picture of a male jumping spider the swollen pedipalps used in sperm transfer are clearly visible on either side of the chelicerae or mouthparts. Jumping spiders have elaborate courtship displays and well developed eyesight.

5. Ghost crabs (*Ocypode*) belong to the order Decapoda, which includes the most advanced crustaeans. Ghost crabs inhabit sandy beaches, attacking any small creatures that venture into their territory. This crab lives on an island off Bermuda and was the subject of an OSF television documentary program.

6. Millipedes grow to almost twelve inches in length and are characterized by the possession of two pairs of legs on each segment, except those right at the front. Despite their name they seldom have more than 130 pairs of legs. Millipedes have biting jaws, which relates them both to insects and, more remotely, to the Crustacea.

5

6

about ten classes, of which the most familiar are, besides the insects, the arachnids – spiders, scorpions and mites; the crustaceans – lobsters, shrimps, crabs, prawns and woodlice; and the myriapods – centipedes, millipedes and symphylans.

Differences between other arthropods and insects

The arachnids are most often confused with insects, but there are two basic differences. The bodies of arachnids are divided into two main portions; those of insects are in three parts. Almost all arachnids have eight legs, while insects have six.

Crustacea are less confusing; almost all crustaceans live in water; a great many of them in the sea. They have two pairs of antennae in front of their mouths. They also, unlike insects, range in size from a water-flea of the genus *Alonella*, which can be less than a hundredth of an inch long, to the giant spider crab (*Machrocheira kaempferi*) of Japan, with a claw-span of up to eight feet.

The crustacean most often confused with an insect is the woodlouse which, though not living in water like most other crustaceans, generally prefers damp places. Since its horny covering, which is generally divided into a series of overlapping plates, is not waterproof, it spends its time shunning sunlight or conditions which would make its body dry out.

Millipedes (class *Diplopoda*), centipedes (*Chilopoda*) and the unfamiliar symphylans and pauropods are grouped together as *Myriapoda*, which means 'many-legged.' Although 'millipede' means 'thousand-legged,' there are only a few species that have more than two hundred. One South African species is said to have 710, but no species is known to have a thousand. Centipedes however do beat their title of 'hundred-legged' for example, one European species, *Himantarum gabrielis*, has up to 154 pairs. Symphylans, a group little studied, mostly have twenty-four legs. They are less than half an inch long. The possession of more than six legs means these animals cannot be insects.

7

8

7. Scorpions are grouped with the spiders and mites in the class Arachnida. The last five segments of the abdomen are constricted to form a tail which ends in a sharp poison sting. Female scorpions like this *Vejovis spinigera* from the south-western United States give birth to live young which, at first, are helpless and must be carried on their mother's back for the first two weeks of life.

8. Zoologists have always been fascinated by *Peripatus*. This curious creature has features that link it both with the segmented annelid worms as well as with the arthropods. Consequently it figures prominently in discussions about the evolutionary history of the arthropods. This species, *P. trinitatis*, comes from Trinidad but close relatives are also found in Africa and New Zealand.

Although insects vary so much in shape, color, habit, and appearance, it is possible to describe a typical insect – a mythical creature somewhat like the Average Man, but useful as a basis for understanding all the many species.

As a rule insects are small, though there are exceptions. Some butterflies and moths have a wingspan up to eleven inches and at least one stick insect (*Pharnacia serratipes*) has a body length of twelve inches. Also notable are some tropical beetles, particularly the goliath beetle (*Goliathus giganteus*) of Equatorial Africa, which has a body nearly six inches long and four inches wide.

But, with few exceptions, insects do not have bulky bodies. This is largely because their method of breathing relies on the diffusion of air through minute tubes known as tracheae. Oxygen from the air filters through these tubes, but the process by which the oxygen penetrates is not efficient over a great distance through tubes as small as insect trachaea.

When considering a typical insect, the first

11

9. Damselflies like this one from Trinidad are fierce predators and swift fliers. Fossil Odonata from the Carboniferous era had wings spanning as much as 23 inches. Damselflies fold their wings together at rest but dragonflies keep theirs spread.

10. Mites are related to spiders and scorpions and are thus not insects. Most species are minute but this velvet mite (*Dinothrombium*) is unusually large and may grow to ⅜ inch in length. It is an inhabitant of deserts and only appears briefly after an occasional rainstorm.

thing to realize is that it is not only inside-out compared with mammals, with its skeleton on the outside – it is also upside-down! Its nervous system runs along the underside of its body, instead of along the backbone. The heart of an insect lies above the digestive tract, while in a vertebrate it lies beneath. Furthermore, its other organs are not always where you might expect to find them. Cicadas, crickets, grasshoppers and many moths have hearing organs, but their location is bizarre. Those of grasshoppers and moths are on the base of the abdomen, while the ears of crickets are on the front legs.

The second point to consider is that many insects change their shapes radically during life. A baby mouse, for example, is a miniature of the adult, however unformed and immature it may be. But an insect goes through an elaborate process known as metamorphosis. Some insects, such as butterflies, go through four stages, in what is called complete metamorphosis: egg, larva (the familiar caterpillar), pupa, adult. Others, such as dragonflies, go through three stages: egg, nymph, adult. Locusts also go through three stages, but the locust nymphs are in the same form as adults when they hatch from the egg, and they develop by molting. An insect with a hard outer casing must discard it if it is to grow, just as a boy in the Middle Ages would have needed a larger suit of armor at eighteen than he did at fourteen.

So, for the sake of simplicity, let us consider our typical insect in its adult form – the form in which most insects are best known, though it may be the shortest period of its life.

Visible components of a typical insect

The skeleton, as we have already seen, is in the form of a tough external case. It is often called the cuticle. It covers every part of the body, even the fine hairs. At the mouth and anus this cuticle turns inwards, and lines part of the digestive system at each end. It also lines the breathing tubes. Owing to its varying uses, the cuticle varies also in its thickness and its hardness. It is extremely thin and therefore more flexible when it is internal.

The body of an insect is divided into three sections: the head, the thorax, and the abdomen. Each is made up of several segments, and the exoskeleton is thin and flexible at the points where the segments join. At other parts it is thick and rigid. At places that will take considerable strain, for example where the muscles are attached, it is reinforced by folding inward.

An insect's head provides its main contact with the world about it. The head carries the eyes, the antennae (feelers), and the feeding organs, which are called mouthparts – they are more complicated than an ordinary mouth as we understand it.

The typical insect uses its mouthparts for biting and chewing. They consist of three sections. First are the mandibles, the main jaws. They work from side to side, and do the bulk of the biting and chewing. Behind the mandibles are the maxillae, a secondary set of jaws whose function varies according to the diet of the insect. In some insects the maxillae hold the food and help in the cutting up. One part of each maxilla is a feeler, called the

9

10

palpus, which may also serve as an organ of taste. Part three of this three-stage mouth is another pair of maxillae, which have become modified to form a labium, a lower lip and include additional palpi. They also help to manipulate the food as the insect chews it. The labrum ,or upper lip, hangs like a flap over the mandibles. In insects which live on liquids the mouth-parts are modified to provide sucking organs.

Insects have two kinds of eyes. There are two compound eyes, one on each side of the head, which consist of many lenses. There are also simple eyes, known as ocelli, usually three in number, which are located between the antennae. The two antennae serve mainly as organs of touch, though bees, for example, are able to smell with their antennae, and mosquitoes hear through them. Eyes and antennae are described in more detail in Chapter 4.

The thorax of our typical insect is in three segments, the prothorax, mesothorax and metathorax. A pair of legs is attached to each segment.

11

In most insects the mesothorax and metathorax each carries a pair of wings.

Insect legs are in five sections. The tarsus is a foot, while the tibia and femur are long sections corresponding to the shin and thigh of a man. Finally, the trochanter and coxa are two short links which join the femur to the thorax.

The wings vary a great deal in form. Flies use their fore wings for flight: their hind wings are small and highly modified as balancing organs. Beetles fly mainly with the rear wings, while the fore wings have become hard, leathery cases to protect the rear wings when the animal is not flying. Bees and wasps use both wings in flight, and lock them together for greater strength. For further details of flight see Chapter 4.

A striking feature of insect wings is the pattern of veins in them. This venation is highly distinctive, and is much used by entomologists to determine the relationship of species and as an aid to identification.

The abdomen of an insect is the largest of the three sections. It contains the heart, the reproductive organs and the digestive system. The abdomen consists of several segments, up to a maximum of eleven. Most of the segments have no external appendages, unlike the segments of the other parts of the body. One segment carries appendages used in mating and egg-laying. Many insects have a rear pair of feelers, called cerci, located either side of the anus.

Inside the insect body

The internal organization of an insect is very different from that of a mammal. Most noticeably, there is only one blood vessel, which runs right along the back of the animal. It consists of a long tube. The rear part is the heart, which beats, and the front part is the aorta, which carries blood to the brain. The blood then flows back through the body of the insect. It fills all the spaces between the other organs, which thus 'float' in a bath of blood. The blood returns to the heart through valves. The blood generally does not carry oxygen,

11. *Pycnopalpa bicordata* is a long-horned grasshopper (Tettigoniidae) from the montane forests of Trinidad. Its features are effectively concealed by subtle markings that make it look like a partly dead leaf. This gives it some measure of protection from predators.

12. The compound eyes of insects are composed of numerous separate ommatidia, each with its own facet. These eyes are extremely sensitive to movement and reach their greatest development in dragonflies (Odonata) and true flies (Diptera). This horsefly has some 20,000 facets in each eye.

13. Butterflies such as this tropical *Opsiphanes* have large wings whose complex patterns are made up from numerous small scales. The mouthparts are modified to form a long proboscis which is used to suck nectar from flowers.

14. In beetles the front pair of wings (elytra) forms a tough shield to protect the membranous hind wings used in flying. *Plusiotis gloriosa* is a scarab that lives on juniper in the mountains of Southern Arizona.

15. Many insects communicate by means of chemical odors. These brush-like antennae belong to a male moth and are used to locate the female at considerable distances by means of the scent she emits.

16. *Stagmatoptera septrionalis* is a praying mantis from Trinidad. Its large eyes enable it to spot its prey at a distance and seize it with its raptorial front legs as soon as the victim comes within range.

17. Weevils are beetles with curiously elongated heads. As can be seen in this palm weevil *Rhina barbirostris* from Trinidad the eyes, antennae and mouthparts are widely separated.

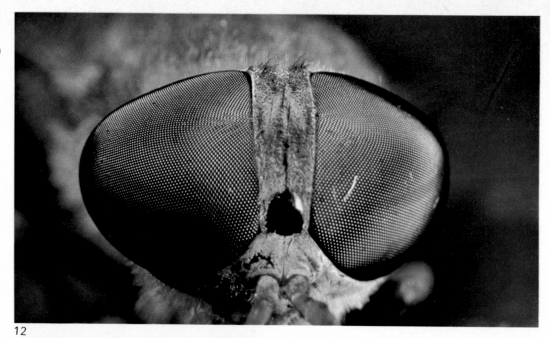

12

13

but merely the nutriment extracted from the insect's food. It is generally green or pale yellow.

The insect obtains its oxygen supply directly from the air. The tracheae, or air-tubes, carry the oxygen all through the body to the various organs.

The alimentary canal is more or less a straight tube, thicker in some parts than others. From the mouth the food passes to the crop, where enzymes break it down. From the crop the food goes through the gizzard to the stomach, where the digested food is absorbed. Waste matter then passes out through the hind intestine. Tubes called Malpighian tubules are attached to the junction of the stomach and hind intestine. They serve as kidneys, removing waste products from the blood. They take their name from Marcello Malpighi, the Italian anatomist who discovered them in the mid-seventeenth century.

Insects have almost the best-developed nervous system of all invertebrates. The only exceptions are the octopus and the squid, which are ocean-dwelling molluscs, and relatives of slugs and snails.

The insect's brain is located in the head, and its principal task is to receive and co-ordinate any information coming through the senses of sight, touch, taste, smell and sound. A nerve cord runs along the lower side of the insect, and on it there are a number of ganglia, or nerve centers. The ganglia control actions and functions in the regions where they are located. So the nervous system of an insect has a much more dispersed control-system than that of, say, a mammal.

The brain exercises overall authority, so to speak, and initiates action. Remove the brain, and the insect will continue to function, but it cannot start any action. The success of the insects as a type is shown by the great length of time they have been around. Arthropods were already in existence some 600 million years ago in what palaeontologists call the Cambrian era. Abundant remains of fossils from this era can be found, and though life certainly existed very much earlier, remains in the rocks are few and difficult to interpret.

Arthropod ancestors

Some of the earliest arthropods belonged to a group known as trilobites, which lived on the muddy bottom of shallow seas. By the time the trilobites became extinct some 230 million years ago the insects were already well established.

The earliest fossil insects date from the Devonian period, which began about 400 million years ago in the middle of the Palaeozoic era.

The first land-living insects were probably wing-less creatures, and it is thought that they may well have been very similar to the silverfish you often find in kitchens and bathrooms. This view is based on the fact that silverfish are among the most primitive of all insects, and are wingless. Other insects show a marked advance in evolution, which reinforces the idea that silverfish are perhaps 'living fossils' – types unchanged for hundreds of millions of years.

Another survival from the past is the mysterious animal known as *Peripatus*, or a velvet worm. It is intermediate in structure between arthropods and

14

15

16

17

the simpler annelids, a group of animals which includes earthworms and leeches. Assuming that animals evolve from the simpler forms to the more complex, the arthropods, including the insects, are a later development than the annelids, and *Peripatus* could be the 'missing link' between them. Although the earliest insects were unable to fly, fossils of flying insects have been found that are around 270 million years old. As these fossils show a considerable advance in structure over the simpler forms, the first winged insects must have existed much earlier than 270 million years ago. These early flying insects are known as Palaeoptera, and they were not unlike the dragonflies of today. Some of them were huge with wingspans of about thirty inches.

With all this time to evolve, it is not surprising that insects are so numerous in species.

The under-explored regions of the world, and in particular the tropics, are teeming with hidden life, and every expedition brings back quantities of preserved specimens for identification. One ardent collector working for ten years in a tropical rain forest could keep the entire entomological staff of a major museum busy for a life-time recording and classifying his finds. This explains why the store-rooms of the world's great natural history museums are full of cases of specimens that have never even been opened, simply because there has not been time to work on their contents.

Classification is a slow and laborious business. The entomologist must look for clues with all the sharpness of mind of a Sherlock Holmes. Outward appearances may help; they may also be decep-tive. Two creatures of comparatively different shape may well prove to have almost identical internal structures, proving that they are really closely related. Others may appear similar, yet prove on close examination to be totally uncon-nected. Some hoverflies for example look re-markably like wasps – but they are flies, none the less, with all the physical characteristics and habits of flies, and none of those of wasps. At moments like this, the question 'What is an insect?' may seem a little difficult to answer.

Chapter 2

Who's Who in the Insect World

There are at least a million known species of insects and entomologists have spent many years classifying them. Even today they do not fully agree, although the broad plan is universally accepted and it is only in matters of detail that there is controversy.

A great many insects have popular names – names that conjure up an instant mental picture. Many names are derived from the insect's appearance, such as the brimstone moth or the blue bug. The red-necked footman earns its name because when it rests it wraps its wings tightly around its body, looking like an old-fashioned footman in livery. Yet other insects are named for what they do: the furniture beetle, for example, is often mis-named the woodworm, and the short-circuit beetle is so known because it eats holes in the lead covering of telephone cables, lets in the damp, and thus causes short circuits.

These names can often be misleading, too. A glow-worm glows, certainly, but it is definitely not a worm. In Britain alone there are twenty-nine species bearing the general name of horseflies, and though some of them have further popular names, even these are shared: four kinds of horseflies are called clegs, for example! And when you remember that there are, worldwide, about 2,500 different species of horsefly, then obviously popular names are not adequate for positive identification.

Classification of insects

Fortunately scientific classification, which sounds formidable, not only solves the problem of different names within the same language, but also the problem of different languages. To a Frenchman, a horsefly might be *un taon* or *un oestre*; to an Italian it would be *un tafano*; to a German *die Pferdebremse*. But entomologists everywhere would recognize the insects as members of the family *Tabanidae*.

In the eighteenth century, when the foundations of modern systematics were laid, the international language of science was Latin. It was the great Swedish botanist, Karl von Linné (Linnaeus), 1707–78, who devised the modern system of nomenclature using a generic followed by a specific name, both in latinized form.

The science of classification is known as *taxonomy*. In taxonomy there are seven basic grades or ranks, each of which defines an animal

19

in more detail according to its characteristics.

This system enables each animal to be pinpointed. Just as an address exactly locates a person, *via* zip code, state, city, street, and street number, so the correct classification identifies an animal. At the same time it relates it to its closest relatives.

The topmost level of the hierarchy is the kingdom. At the moment two kingdoms, animal and plant, are recognized, though there is a growing recognition by scientists that some organisms on the borderline between animals and plants, such as bacteria, should have a kingdom of their own, called Protista.

The main divisions of the animal kingdom are phyla, of which there are some twenty-five. The actual number, however, depends on which classification system is used.

Each phylum is divided into several classes, each class including animals with the same basic characteristics. Insects form the class Insecta within the phylum Arthropoda. Each class is then divided into orders, which are groups that are even more closely related. Unfortunately, entomologists do not wholly agree on the number of orders in the insect world. Some tend to unite such diverse groups as the stick insects and grass-

18. *Adejeania vexatrix* is a two-winged fly (Diptera) that feeds on alpine flowers above 7,200 feet in the mountains of southern Arizona. Like other members of the family Tachinidae the larval stages of this fly are parasitic in caterpillars and other insects.

19. The most primitive insects do not possess wings. This springtail (Collembola) lives in soil and leaf litter. If attacked it is able to jump by means of a special organ beneath its abdomen.

20

21

22

24

23

hoppers into a single order while others prefer to split such groups into smaller, more homogeneous units. In this book we largely follow the classification given in the ninth edition of Dr A. D. Imms's *General Textbook of Entomology*, one of the great standard works on the subject, and divide the world of insects into twenty-nine orders. These twenty-nine orders are briefly listed in the chart on page 22 and described in more detail thereafter.

The orders are divided into families, and here we are getting on to much more familiar ground. For example, the horseflies mentioned earlier form the family *Tabanidae*. Family names end in the letters *-idae*. Subfamilies end in *-inae*.

Finally we come down to the last two divisions, the genus (plural genera) and the species. These may be thought of as last name and first name respectively. A genus is a group of closely related creatures within a family, while the species is the final division, all of whose members are alike and can interbreed.

When a zoologist refers to any animal he uses

25

26

20. Although cockroaches are most often found in buildings, the majority of species live away from man, very often in leaf litter on the forest floor. *Panchlora cubensis* is a tropical species that is active at night on tree trunks.

21. This tropical *Kolla* species belongs to the family of Hemiptera or true bugs that are known as leaf hoppers (Cicadellidae). They feed on plant juices and can leap a considerable distance if disturbed.

22. The hawkmoths (Sphingidae) form a large and widely distributed family of readily recognizable Lepidoptera. They are powerful fliers and some can suck nectar from flowers while on the wing. *Amplyterus gamascus* is one of more than 80 species that occur on the island of Trinidad.

23. Members of the family Flatidae are found mainly in tropical areas and like most other hemipterans they feed on plant juices. The prominent tail is in fact a tuft of fine waxy filaments which the insect secretes.

24. Despite this insect's appearance it is not a wasp. Its long ovipositor indicates that it is a parasitic hymenopteran belonging to the family Ichneumonidae, which do not possess a sting. Mimicry of this sort, in which a harmless animal assumes the livery of a dangerous or distasteful one, is common amongst insects.

25. Coreid bugs belong to the suborder Heteroptera in which the fore wings are membranous at the top but thicker and harder towards the front. They feed on plant juices and many species emit a powerful and most unpleasant smell.

26. *Dinia mena* is a clearwing moth from the montane forests of Trinidad. The most striking characteristic of these moths is the absence of scales on most of the wing area. Many species are very bee- or wasp-like in appearance.

the genus and species names together. By long-established convention the genus name takes a capital letter and the species does not, and both are always in italics.

In the world of insects an understanding of the way they are named is especially important, because the vast majority of insects have no popular name, only a Latin one.

Ideally, the Latin genus and species name should have a meaning that conveys something about the insect. The perfect example is *Apis mellifera*, the honey bee. *Apis* means bee, and *mellifera* means honey-producing. Still among the bees, *Bombus* the name of the genus to which bumblebees belong, means booming or buzzing, while the flower bees, *Anthophora*, derive their name from the Greek word *anthos*, flower. This well illustrates the point that a great many scientific names are in a latinized form of Greek.

To maintain some sort of order in these names, zoologists have established an International Commission on Zoological Nomenclature, which

27

28

29

30

31

attempts to settle all disputes over what animals should be called. If more than one name has been coined for a creature, then in general the oldest name is the one that has priority.

The full, formal placing of a honey bee, below, shows how the classification system works.

Kingdom: Animalia
Phylum: Arthropoda
Class: Insecta
Subclass: Pterygota
Order: Hymenoptera
Suborder: Apocrita
Superfamily: Apoidea
Family: Apidae
Subfamily: Apinae
Tribe: Apini
Genus: Apis
Species: mellifera

It will be noticed that this list includes three categories not previously mentioned, subclass, suborder and tribe. Other intermediate groupings sometimes met with include subphylum, super-

32

33

27. The beetles form the largest order in the entire animal kingdom with more than a quarter of a million described species. The scarabs, like this species from Georgia, form a large and distinctive family, many of whose members are very brightly colored.

28. The ants are social hymenopterans with a well differentiated caste structure. Within the colony particular tasks are performed by specialized individuals. Many ants have established associations with plant-eating insects such as aphids which excrete a sweet liquid that the ants feed on.

29. More than 600 species of swallowtail butterfly (Papilionidae) are known, the majority of them from the tropics. The majority of these large and brightly colored insects are readily recognized by conspicuous tail-like projections from the hind wings.

30. *Brenthus* belongs to a predominantly tropical family of curiously elongated beetles whose larval stages are spent boring in timber. The mouthparts are very small and are carried at the end of a greatly elongated rostrum, rather like that of their weevil relatives.

31. The palm weevil, *Rhina barbirostris*, is a large beetle that causes extensive damage to the plantations of coconut palms in Trinidad. The larvae burrow into the trunk, thus killing the tree.

32. *Chrysis ignita* is one of the commonest and most beautiful of the British cuckoo wasps (Chrysididae). They fly only in hot, bright sunshine and are often found near the nests of various solitary bees and wasps upon which they are parasitic.

33. *Aegithus* belongs to the beetle family Erotylidae and like most of its relatives comes from South America. The larval stage of these beetles is passed in the fruiting bodies of fungi.

class, infraclass, cohort, subgenus and subspecies. But for all practical purposes the categories that matter are the seven basic ones of kingdom, phylum, class, order, family, genus and species. The additional divisions are useful when classifying a very large group of related animals which needs to be broken down into manageable sections.

In the case of insects there are two subclasses which reflect a basic difference: whether the animal has wings or not. The Apterygota (from two Greek words meaning 'without wings') are insects that have never in their evolutionary history had wings. The Pterygota ('winged') are insects with wings, though some of them, such as fleas and lice and the female worker ants, may have become secondarily wingless in the course of evolution.

The Pterygota are again subdivided into two groups: the Exopterygota, which have a simple three-stage metamorphosis, and the Endopterygota, which have a complex four-stage metamorphosis (described in Chapter 3).

The orders at a glance

Apterygota – wingless insects	
Thysanura	Silverfish
Diplura	Two-pronged bristletails
Protura	Minute, blind soil-dwellers – no common name
Collembola	Springtails
Pterygota – insects with wings	
(1) *Exopterygota*	
Ephemeroptera	Mayflies
Odonata	Dragonflies and damselflies
Plecoptera	Stoneflies
Grylloblattodea	Obscure soil-living insects – no common name
Orthoptera	Crickets, grasshoppers
Phasmida	Stick and leaf insects
Dermaptera	Earwigs
Embioptera	Web-spinners
Dictyoptera	Cockroaches
Isoptera	Termites
Zoraptera	Rare minute tropical insects – no common name
Psocoptera	Booklice
Mallophaga	Biting lice
Anoplura	Sucking lice
Hemiptera	True bugs
Thysanoptera	Thrips
(2) *Endopterygota*	
Neuroptera	Alder, snake and lacewing flies
Mecoptera	Scorpionflies
Lepidoptera	Butterflies and moths
Trichoptera	Caddis flies
Diptera	True flies
Siphonaptera	Fleas
Hymenoptera	Bees, wasps, ants, sawflies
Coleoptera	Beetles
Strepsiptera	Stylopids

34

35

Thysanura The common name for all these wingless insects is 'three-pronged bristletail' and their Latin name comes from the Greek *thysanos*, fringe, and *oura*, tail. They have three tail-like filaments at the rear. The most familiar species is the silverfish, which is common in kitchens. It is drawn there by the starchy and sugary foods. However, most of the 350 species live in forests, in dead or decaying matter such as rotting wood and leaves, or in the soil. The largest is no more than one inch long.

Diplura These are the two-pronged bristletails, and the name of their order comes from the Greek *diplos*, double, and *oura*, tail. They have no wings or eyes, and spend their lives in dark, dank places feeding on decaying matter. Most of the 400 species are very small, but one, *Heterojapyx souli* of Australia, can be up to two inches long. These bristletails are the most primitive of all the insects; and internally they are like symphylans, the small relatives of the centipedes and millipedes.

Protura These wingless insects are so small and unobtrusive that they escaped notice until 1907. The name means 'simple tail' because the animals' bodies end in a telson, or pointed rear segment – hence their only popular name, telson-tails. They have no eyes and no antennae, but use their front pair of legs as feelers. They are whitish in color, and live in the ground in damp places. The largest of the fifty known species is barely eight hundredths of an inch long, and most are much smaller.

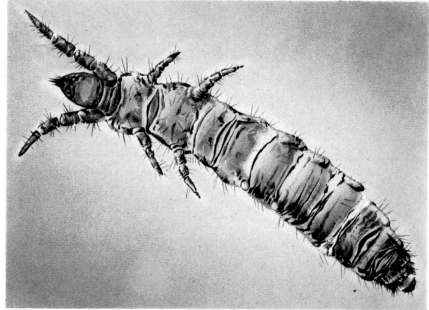

36

Collembola These insects, in the fourth of the wingless orders, are popularly known as springtails, because most of them have a rear forked jumping organ. This organ, or spring, is normally hooked forward under the body: when released it propels the insect forward about an inch. About 1,500 species are known, and in moist ground they are often extremely numerous. It has been estimated that two acres of ground can hold as many as 500 million springtails – yet few people would notice them. The largest springtails are about two tenths of an inch long, and they vary greatly in color. The name Collembola comes from the Greek *kolla*, glue, and *embolon*, a peg, and refers to a tube on the underside which was believed to emit a sticky substance. It is now thought to absorb moisture.

37

38

Ephemeroptera The mayflies which form this order have a truly ephemeral existence – hence their name, which comes from the Greek *ephemeros*, living a day, and *pteron*, wing. Altogether, a mayfly's life may be as long as four years, but most of it is spent as a larva or nymph living in a stream or pool. The adult mayfly finally emerges when the nymph floats to the surface. There the males perform a wild mating dance near the water. As each female flies into the cloud of dancing males she is seized and mates in mid-air. She lays her eggs in the water, and then dies. The adult life span is never more than a week, and may be only a few hours. In its adult form, the mayfly does not eat. Mayfly nymphs vary in their life-style, some staying in running water, others burrowing deep into the mud or the banks of the pool or stream. There are about 1,400 species.

Odonata The 4,500 species of this order are commonly called dragonflies and damselflies. The damselflies, which have two pairs of almost identical wings, form the suborder Zygoptera. Dragonflies, however, have hind wings broader than the front ones and they form the suborder Anisoptera. There is also a third, intermediate, suborder, Anisozygoptera. Only two living species of this suborder are known, one in Japan and one in India, but there are many fossil types. The nymphs of dragonflies and damselflies live in water, but the adults fly considerable distances away from it. Dragonflies are particularly strong fliers. All species are carnivores and eat mosquitoes and small flies, which they catch on the wing. In mating the male grips the female around the neck with his tail claspers, while she curves her long abdomen around to touch his, thus forming a wheel. Some species actually mate in flight in this position. The name Odonata, which means toothed, refers to the strong teeth on their mandibles.

39

Plecoptera These are the stoneflies, which lead quiet, secluded lives, first as nymphs in streams, then as adults crawling among riverbank stones – hence their popular name. Their scientific name comes from the Greek *plekein*, to fold, and *pteron*, wing, because their wings are folded flat when at rest. These unobtrusive insects are known to few except anglers and entomologists. They range from brown to light green in color, and vary in size from wingspans of one to two inches. The adults do not fly very well, and mostly run for cover if disturbed. Though they do not feed, they may live up to six months.

40

41

Grylloblattodea These rare insects are apparently living fossils, survivors of the common ancestors of grasshoppers, cockroaches, mantises and stick insects. They like a cool life just above the treeline on mountains, and have been found in North America, the Soviet Union and Japan. Only six species are so far known. They are largely nocturnal and feed as scavengers.

Orthoptera The 10,000 species of this large order, which gets its name from the Greek *orthos*, straight, and *pteron*, wing, are the grasshoppers, crickets, mole-crickets, katydids and locusts. Most of them can jump, using their long and powerful hind legs, and though most can fly they prefer leaping. From this comes the alternative name of the order, Saltatoria, from the Latin *saltare*, to leap. However, the Orthoptera are probably best known by their voices. In nearly every species it is only the males who 'sing,' but both sexes have good hearing organs. The short-horned grasshoppers, which include locusts, have scrapers on their hind legs and files on the fore-wings. Long-horned grasshoppers, katydids and crickets have both file and scraper on the wings. The sound is amplified by lifting the forewings slightly and forming a small resonant cavity. Mole-crickets, as their name implies, spend a large part of their lives underground. Their forelegs are adapted to digging.

42

Phasmida The insects of this order are noted for their resemblance to plant life, and comprise the walking sticks or stick insects, and the leaf insects. They vary greatly in size, from around one inch to a record thirteen inches – the longest insect known. They are most abundant in the tropical rain forests of Asia, where they feed on vegetation, and are active mostly at night. By day they cling to plants, hanging motionless in an almost cataleptic trance, a reflex action known as thanatosis. Some species have no wings, while in others only the males have wings. It is common for them to reproduce by parthenogenesis – that is, by eggs that have not been fertilized by a male. Males are rare, and in some species appear to be completely absent. But such males as there are live longer than the females. The 'moving leaf' insects of southern Asia rely on their wings for their leaf-like appearance, but only the rare males can fly. All the Phasmids rely on their camouflage for protection, for they move extremely slowly.

44   43

Dermaptera This order, with about a thousand known species, contains the earwigs. The name of their order comes from the Greek word *derma*, skin. Their popular name is connected with the ear in French, German and other languages besides English. The bodies of earwigs end with a formidable-looking pair of pincers, similar to the tool once used for ear-piercing. They like to hide in crevices, and have been known to use human ears for this purpose. Earwigs spend their lives in dark, damp places, foraging at night. Their diet consists of fruit and vegetable matter, and some of them eat other arthropods and their larvae; many are scavengers. Some species have no wings, and all but one are poor fliers.

45

Embioptera These small insects live in tunnels of woven silk, which they spin with their feet using a secretion from glands in the front legs. They are called web-spinners, and only about 150 species are known, mostly from the tropics. They make their homes in dark places under stones and bark, usually in colonies. They eat various dead and decaying vegetable matter, feeding at night. All the females are wingless, but some males can fly; however, when disturbed they all choose to run for safety even if they can fly. The name of their order comes from the Greek *embios*, lively, and *pteron*, wing. Owing to their secretive habits few people ever see them.

46

47

Dictyoptera This order comprises cockroaches and praying mantises, of which there are about 5,500 species. Cockroaches have flat oval bodies, ranging in length from a few hundreds of an inch to three inches. In prehistoric times, cockroaches were among the first insects to fly but today, though some species still have wings, they run rather than fly. Some species like to share our homes and food, but most species live out of doors in a variety of habitats.

The praying mantis looks much more like a grasshopper than a cockroach. When threatened it raises itself up with its huge, powerful forelegs held in an apparently devotional attitude. But its appearance is deceptive; it is in fact waiting to pounce. When it does so the pincers of the front legs open and close like lightning to seize the prey.

Mantises are carnivores. The larger species attack even mice, frogs, and small birds. The males are smaller than the females, and it is not uncommon for the female to eat the male in the act of mating, or immediately after.

Isoptera This name, meaning 'equal wings,' refers to the termites. These highly organized social insects are often called white ants, because they are pale-colored and live in vast colonies like ants. There the resemblance ends, because the bodies of termites are much less highly developed than those of ants. In fact their nearest relatives are the cockroaches. The 2,000 or so species are found largely in the tropics, or in warm temperate climates. Termites must keep their bodies moist, so they build their homes in soil or rotting wood. Some species eat wood, some rotted organic material, and some practically anything. A termite colony may contain up to a million individuals. Many species live in tall mounds with tunnels leading into the ground. A few species, however, build nests high in trees. The colony is headed by a queen, who is much larger than the other residents and may live for twenty years or more, laying eggs. The king is also long-lived. Workers and soldiers live for about four years.

Zoraptera These minute insects are mostly very tiny. They were discovered in 1913, but they have not so far acquired a popular name. They live mainly in hot, humid regions, and only about twenty-five species are known. Their nearest relatives are the termites, and like them they need moist living quarters. They make their homes in the ground or in rotting tree stumps, and form small colonies. Only some have wings. The name of the order comes from the Greek *zoros*, pure, and *aptera*, wingless, because the first recorded species was wingless.

48

Psocoptera These delicate insects are known variously, according to their eating habits, as booklice, barklice, or dustlice. Some of the 1,600 species look like lice, but they have long antennae and are not parasites. Others look like jumping plant lice, which belong to the true bugs (order Hemiptera). The psocids, as they are called, are mostly less than an eighth of an inch long. Some have large wings, some small ones and some none at all. The order was discovered in 1701, and came to light as a result of the ticking noise made by booklice in an English library. Species make their homes in forests, in the nests of bees, wasps, ants, and birds, and on leaves and the bark of trees. Their name comes from a Greek word meaning to grind to pieces, plus *pteron*, wing.

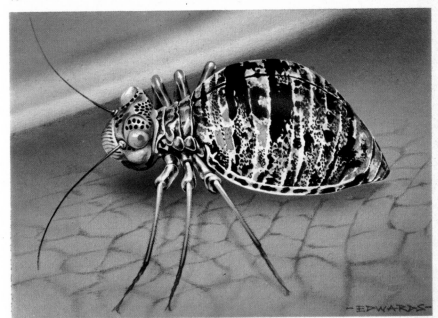

49

50

Mallophaga These are the chewing or biting lice, which like the sucking lice of the order Anoplura are parasites. The chewing lice get their name from two Greek words meaning 'wool biting,' and their lives are spent on the bodies of mammals and birds, eating not only wool but feathers, hair, scales and fatty excretion from the skin. They range in color from yellow through red to black, and have flat, oval bodies. They have no wings. The largest are about an eighth of an inch long, but some species are much smaller. Each of the more than 2,600 species is adapted to life on one particular kind of host animal. Some live on just one part of the host, and none can survive long on a different kind of host. When the host dies, these parasites generally die too, unless they are lucky enough to transfer to another host in time. Birds are the favored hosts; even Antarctic pelicans are infested. To keep their hold on their hosts the biting lice grip the hair or feathers with the claws on the ends of their feet.

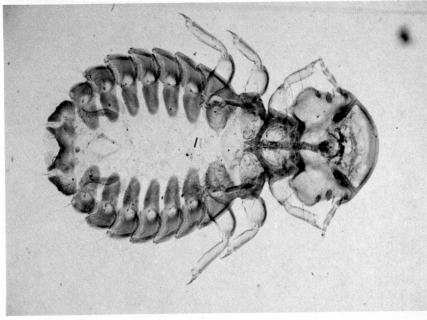

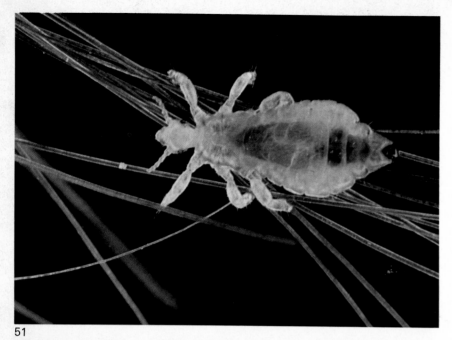

51

Anoplura This order, whose name comes from the Greek words *anoplos*, unarmed, and *oura*, a tail, are often more graphically described as Siphunculata, or sucking lice. About 250 species of sucking lice are known, and they all live as parasites on mammals, whose blood provides their food. Each species of sucking lice lives as a rule on only one type of mammal. One species, for example, is found only on elephants, another only on seals. Two species infest human beings, and closely related ones live on apes, man's nearest relatives in the animal world. The human louse, *Pediculus humanus*, occurs in two distinct forms, one living in the hair of the head, the other on the rest of the body. The crab louse, *Pthirus pubis*, lives in the pubic hair; as far as is known this louse does not carry disease. Most sucking lice are about one tenth of an inch long, and a good meal would be a tiny drop of blood. The insect injects saliva to prevent the blood from clotting quickly; this facilitates sucking. The sticky eggs cling to the host's hair, skin, or clothing.

52

53

Hemiptera The layman uses the word 'bug' for any insect, but to the entomologist the Hemiptera are the only insects to which the term properly applies. This is a large order of around 50,000 known species. Zoologists divide it into two suborders, Heteroptera and Homoptera. They all have mouthparts designed for both piercing and sucking, contained in a long, slender rostrum or beak on the underside of the body. The bugs vary in size from a few hundredths of an inch to more than four inches long. Their generally flat backs are covered with scales and plates in colors ranging from black to metallic-looking gold. The name Heteroptera means 'different wings,' because the front wings have tough, leathery roots and thin, translucent tips. With wings folded the insects appear to have only half of each wing – hence the order name, Hemiptera, meaning 'half-wings.'

Homoptera have front wings that are uniform in structure. They live by sucking the juices of plants, and many of them excrete honeydew. They include cicadas, aphids and scale insects.

Thysanoptera The members of this order have the common name of thrips; they are also called bladder-footed insects, having bladder-like organs on their feet which enable them to get a grip on smooth surfaces. Their order name means 'fringed wings' and describes their distinctive wings. These are fringed with bristle-like projections which effectively double the surface area. There are about 3,000 species, ranging in size from a quarter of an inch down to a few thousandths of an inch. Owing to their small size they are hardly ever seen, but they can often be felt in hot, thundery weather, when swarms of winged species take to the air and irritate people's hands and faces. Most thrips feed by sucking the sap from plants. Some are predatory on mites and other insects, including aphids and larger thrips.

Neuroptera Members of this order have two pairs of large, translucent wings which they hold over their bodies like a tent when at rest. The pattern of veins in the wings resembles the finest lace, and from this comes their order name, which means 'nerve-winged'. But even with these beautiful wings, neuropterans are weak fliers. There are about 4,000 species of these soft-bodied insects. Most of them feed on other soft-bodied insects, such as aphids and thrips. They spend nearly all their lives in the larval stage; most have only a brief adult life. The larvae of some species are called aphidlions because they prey on aphids from which they suck the blood through hollow sickle-shaped jaws until only shriveled carcasses remain. There are several major kinds of neuropterans. Alderflies live in and near water and include the large dobsonflies of North America. Snakeflies have a greatly elongated section of the thorax which looks like a long neck. Antlions look somewhat like dragonflies when at rest. Lacewings are perhaps the best-known members of the order.

54

Mecoptera The order name comes from the Greek *mekos*, length, and *pteron*, wing, and refers to their long and narrow wings. Their popular name, scorpionflies, derives from the fact that the males of one family carry their genitalia curved up and over their backs like the tail of a scorpion. The elongate head is at right angles to the body so that the chewing mouthparts point downwards. The immature scorpionflies live on small dead insects and other carrion, and the adults add nectar and fruit to their diet. Scorpionflies spend most of their lives in or on the soil, and even the adults do not fly very much. Some species, living in cold northern climates, have only vestigial wings, and hop like grasshoppers. Altogether there are only about 300 known species of scorpionflies, but they are a very old-established group. Some fossil specimens 250 million years old are almost identical to existing species.

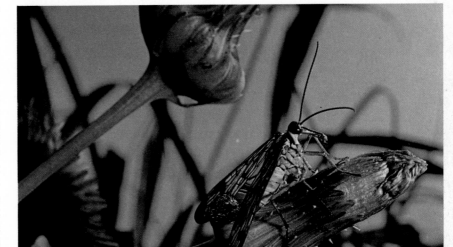

55   56

Lepidoptera The insects of this order are the butterflies and moths, perhaps the most beautiful of all insects. The order name comes from the Greek words *lepis*, a scale, and *pteron*, wing. The wings of butterflies and moths are indeed covered with tiny scales which build up like a miniature mosaic picture to produce the often vivid coloring associated with these insects. The Lepidoptera form one of the biggest orders, with more than 100,000 known species. They range in size from the pigmy moth, *Nepticula microtheriella*, with a wingspan of a sixteenth of an inch, to the giant birdwing butterfly, whose is over a foot.

Most adult butterflies and moths have a long proboscis or sucking tube which is uncurled to suck nectar from deep inside a flower. Some of the hawk moths have prosboces more than eleven inches long. The typical caterpillar (larval stage) has eight pairs of legs – three on the thorax like the adult insect, plus five on the abdomen. Some caterpillars spin cocoons, from silk. Man uses silk from the mulberry silkworm, *Bombyx mori*.

57

Trichoptera These insects are the caddis flies, dull-colored insects which are often mistaken for moths. They are generally found near water, in which the larvae live. The name of the order comes from the Greek *thrix*, a hair, and *pteron*, wing, and both body and wings are covered with very fine hairs. A few species have scales on the wings like those of butterflies. The eggs are laid on or by water, and the larvae, which are soft-bodied animals known as caddis worms, build themselves cases for protection. Their main material is a sticky thread, to which the larva attaches grains of sand, seeds, small shells, leaves or twigs. There are about 3,000 species of caddis flies.

58

59

Diptera These are the two-winged flies, and their name comes from the Greek *di*, two, and *pteron*, wing. They are often called true flies to distinguish them from all the other insects that have 'fly' as part of their common names. Their distinctive features are the possession of only two functional wings; the two halteres, small clubbed growths, are all that remain of the hind wings. There are at least 70,000 known species, including the familiar sturdy-bodied houseflies and blowflies or bluebottles; the more delicate craneflies, mosquitoes and gnats; the wasp-like hoverflies; and many other flies which have diverse shapes and colors. They exploit many sources of food, mostly in liquid form. Some flies are carriers of disease, but many species pollinate flowers and perform a valuable task as scavengers. The legless larvae are known as maggots, or grubs and they include woodborers, leaf miners, stem and root-borers, internal parasites and feeders on decaying organic matter.

Siphonaptera These are the fleas, which suck blood from mammals and birds. The order is also known as Aphaniptera, from the Greek *aphanes*. not apparent, and *pteron*, wing, because these insects are wingless. Fleas live as parasites in the adult stage, but feed as larvae on waste material, including the droppings of adult fleas. The adults have powerful legs which enable them to leap great distances in relation to their size. The common flea, *Pulex irritans*, can jump 130 times its own height. Their ability to leap so well enables fleas to change hosts if they need to, and unlike lice they can survive away from their host for long periods. Fleas are major carriers of disease, most notably plague.

Hymenoptera This huge order of at least 100,000 species includes wasps, bees, ants, sawflies and many parasites, both large and small. The name comes from the Greek *hymen*, a membrane, and *pteron*, wing, though these insects are not the only one with membranous wings. The order is divided into two suborders. The Symphyta contains the sawflies and wood-wasps, which have no 'waist.' Insects of the other suborder, Apocrita, have a narrow 'waist' between thorax and abdomen — seen most clearly on a wasp. The larvae of the Symphyta are mainly leaf eaters or borers. The adults either do not feed at all or consume nectar and pollen. The Apocrita are divided into two groups. The Parasitica are mostly parasites, a hundredth of an inch to four inches in length.

The Aculeata include the ants, bees and wasps. Some of the species are solitary insects, such as the solitary wasps or the solitary bees, while the bumblebees start their colonies anew each spring. The social bees, wasps and ants live in highly organized societies (see Chapter 6).

60

Coleoptera These are the beetles, which form the largest order, with more than 250,000 species. They range in size from less than two tenths of an inch in length to giants up to five inches long, weighing three and a half ounces. The name Coleoptera comes from the Greek *coleos*, a sheath, and *pteron*, wing, and describes one of the beetle's prime characteristics: the front wings are hard or leathery and come together over the back to protect the thin, membranous hind wings which are used in flight. A few species have no flying wings at all. The hard front wings are called *elytra*, from another Greek word meaning sheath. In most species they provide lift but no propulsion in flight. Beetles have biting mouthparts and feed on a very wide range of foods. Some species are carnivorous and some are carrion feeders. However, the majority feed on plant material, either living or dead. Many species have become pests, feeding on grain, hides, clothes and carpets. This order includes sexton beetles, stag beetles, glow-worms, deathwatch beetles and ladybugs.

61

Strepsiptera The members of this small order of about 400 species are known as the twisted-wing parasites. The name of the order comes from the Greek *strepsis*, twisting, and *pteron*, wing. They are very small; their larvae are parasites on the larvae of other insects such as bees, wasps and plant hoppers. The females are wingless.

62

Chapter 3

Reproduction and Development

Hans Andersen enchanted the world with his story of the Ugly Duckling which grew up to be a beautiful, graceful swan. But the change from drab cygnet to snow-white swan is far less dramatic than the changes experienced by countless insects. These insects have a complex life story which ends in the appearance of the adult form of the insects. And the adults' only purpose is to reproduce the species. Indeed, insects such as mayflies and wild silk moths in the adult form do not even feed, but mate, lay eggs and die, often within a few hours.

Many of the basic principles of insect reproduction are similar to those of other animals. A female insect possesses a pair of ovaries in which the eggs are produced. From the ovaries the eggs pass to the vagina, in which they are fertilized by sperm from the male. The male has a pair of testes in which the sperm is produced. From the testes the sperm cells pass down sperm ducts to the ejaculatory duct which runs through an intromittant organ, the aedeagus.

At this point similarities with higher animals end and the diversity that characterizes so much of insect life takes over. Some females have a pouch, the *bursa copulatrix*. The sperm cells pass into this instead of directly into the vagina. In viviparous insects such as tsetse flies part of the genital duct is enlarged to form a uterus for the developing larva. In most insects, such as the queen honey bee, the sperm is stored in a spermbank, the *spermatheca* from which sperm cells are released as required. Although the queen bee mates only once, she can go on producing fertile eggs for up to five years. In most Hymenoptera the female lays a fertilized egg to produce a female and an unfertilized egg to produce a male. But the male is not completely essential in the insect world. Many insects can reproduce by parthenogenesis, which literally means virgin birth. In this case the unfertilized egg gives rise to a female. There are some insect species in which males have never been found; in other species males occur only at certain times of the year. During the summer aphids produce many generations with no males, the females giving birth not to eggs like most insects but to live young. Towards autumn males are produced again, and the aphids of that generation mate in the ordinary way. The females then lay fertilized wintering-over eggs, which hatch in the spring,

64

when the cycle of virgin births starts all over again.

Aphids, as we have seen, produce several generations every year. By contrast the periodical cicada, *Magicicada septendecim*, of the United States has a life cycle of seventeen years from egg to adult, most of which is passed underground.

The life cycle of nearly all insects begins with the fundamental problem of finding a mate. The variety of courtship rituals and devices is apparently never-ending, but for the vast majority of insects the ability to fly is one of the essentials, and even in species where the females cannot fly the males generally have wings to seek them out.

All the animal senses are called into play during courtship, but probably the most important is the one we know as smell. Smell plays a comparatively small part in the life of the human race, so it is difficult for us to imagine what an important role it takes in the lives of many animals.

A great many insects, and other animals, use smells for communication, particularly between the sexes. These smells are chemical substances which have been given the general name of pheromones. Courting insects have an amazing ability to detect pheromones, sometimes over distances of many miles. This phenomenon was observed and described by the great French

63, 64. *Antheraea pernyi* is one of the wild silk moths (Saturniidae). When the female emerges she waits until the evening and then disseminates scent which the male can detect downwind for a distance of a mile or so by means of his elaborate antennae (64). The male flies to the female and they mate (63). The following two nights the female lays her eggs. These moths cannot feed and within a week both sexes are dead.

33

65

66

67

34

naturalist Jean Henri Fabre more than seventy years ago, long before pheromones were identified or named. He kept a female oak eggar moth, *Lasiocampa quercus*, in a wire-gauze cage, surrounded by a dozen saucers each of which contained a powerful-smelling substance. This barrage of smells included naphthalene, oil of lavender, gasoline, and hydrogen sulphide. Fabre's laboratory already smelled strongly of the tobacco he smoked. The pheromones from the female moth, undetectable to the human nose, lured males from all around; moreover, many of the males flew in with the wind, indicating that the scent of the female had traveled up-wind.

Many male butterflies and moths also produce pheromones which excite the female and induce her to accept her mate – in much the same way, if we are to believe the advertisements, as do certain brands of after-shave lotion. Examples of males with a sexy smell are the appropriately-named satyr butterflies, most of which have fairly dull coloring of brown or black. The grayling, *Eumenis semele*, which comes from the same family, has a courtship ritual in which the scent scales on the male's wings rub against the antennae of the female.

Audio and visual courtship

Many other insects, however, find a mate with the aid of sound. For example, the female mosquito emits a note of around 500 cycles per second – a little sharper than B natural in the middle of the piano. This noise, which will send humans diving for cover, attracts the male mosquito; momentarily, a tuning-fork of the same pitch will attract them too.

The noisiest and most familiar of the insects that serenade their mates are the crickets and grasshoppers of the order Orthoptera, and the cicadas of the order Hemiptera. A few families of the Orthoptera are exceptions, and are silent; a few females can produce sounds. But generally it is the males which 'sing.' Grasshoppers produce their sounds by rubbing a file on their hind legs against a scraper on part of their wing covers. They sing louder and more rapidly the higher the temperature of the air around them. The nature of the song varies according to the desired effect. A group of males will sing together in chorus, though their song is one of rivalry; each one is trying to attract a female and shout the others down. When a male has located a female, and generally the females come flocking, attracted by the noise, he switches to a quieter wooing song calculated to excite the female until mating begins.

To pick up all this sound, the short-horned grasshoppers have their ears either on the last segment of the thorax or on the first segment of the abdomen. But the long-horned grasshoppers and the crickets have their ears in an even more bizarre location, on their front legs, and they can swing their legs, like an adjustable radio aerial, in order to locate the direction from which the sound is coming.

Noisy though the grasshoppers and crickets can be, they are out-voiced by the sound produced by cicadas. The cicada's voice is produced by a pair of drum-like membranes in the insect's abdomen.

68

69

70

71

65. *Dynastes hercules* are seen here about to mate.

66. These mating stick insects are active only at night; during the day they remain motionless and are difficult to find.

67. The fruit fly, *Drosophila*, like most insects lays its eggs on food which is suitable for the development of its young.

68. *Pieris brassicae*, the cabbage white butterfly, lays 60–100 yellow eggs on the lower surface of a cabbage leaf or other member of the Brassica family.

69. Typically the cockroach ootheca is divided into two rows of pockets by a longitudinal partition and each egg occupies a pocket. The pronymphs hatch by forcing open the valves of the envelope and wriggling free. They at once molt into first instar nymphs.

70. The eggs of the female cockroach are enclosed in a horny capsule or ootheca which is carried protruding from the mother's body for several days before being placed on a blob of sticky secretion and carefully covered with debris.

71. The praying mantis lays 40 or so eggs in a frothy secretion which rapidly hardens to a spongy texture and forms the egg case. Although mantid eggs may be well protected against birds and lizards they are nevertheless parasitized by various hymenopterans.

A muscle attached to the membrane causes it to distort with a click and so produce a vibration which causes the sound. The noise is amplified by two larger cavities which lie close to the drums. These act as a resonating apparatus; without it the cicada can still sing, but not so loudly. At mating time the males 'sing' to attract the females. The males themselves have hearing organs, but these are out of action when the cicadas are singing, presumably because the noise of their own voices would be unbearable.

Sight is much used as an aid to courtship, particularly by those insects such as flies which have good eyes. Insects such as stoneflies, caddis flies and many midges indulge in a mating dance performed by a great swarm of males together. The dance attracts the females to them. Sight also helps identification, even in species where it is reinforced by pheromones.

However, the most interesting visual aid to courtship is provided by the light emitted by fireflies and glow-worms, which are beetles of the

72

73

72. Certain pentatomid bugs, of which this Trinidad species is one, exhibit maternal care. The female rests in a brooding attitude over the eggs and remains in close proximity to the young for several days after they hatch.

73. The wasp *Bembix integra* scrapes back sand to uncover the entrance to her tunnel. Several times daily she visits her larva to determine whether it needs more food; if it does, she departs to catch and bring back a fly. The tunnel entrance is always camouflaged with sand except when the wasp is below ground. The wasp looks after several tunnels, containing larvae of different ages, at the same time. In its use of progressive feeding *Bembix* differs from almost all other solitary wasps.

74. *Sphex albisectus* is a solitary wasp that first excavates a vertical shaft in the ground. She then finds and paralyzes a grasshopper and drags it back to her tunnel. The wasp enters the tunnel, turns around, reaches out to seize her prey and pulls it down the shaft. After laying an egg on the insect she fills in the tunnel until there is no evidence of its existence.

74

75

families Lampyridae and Elateridae. The beetles are nocturnal, and in a great many of the species the females are wingless – hence their familiar name of glow-worms. The female positions herself on the ground or on a plant so that her light shines clearly. The male, who emits a fainter light, flies around in search of a possible mate. When many males are flying at the same time the air is filled with tiny sparks of light. When a male approaches, the female glows more brightly. Most of the Lampyridae flash on and off, and signal to each other in a pre-determined code. The light produced is a cold light, like that from a fluorescent tube, and it is caused by a chemical reaction.

The Elateridae have two kinds of light. When in flight they produce an orange light, and when at rest they flash a green light. Both sexes are winged and produce light.

There are other light-producing insects which go under the general name of glow-worms, including the larvae of some beetles and gnats; but their lights do not seem to be connected with courtship. They include the railroad worm, a beetle belonging to the genus *Phrixothrix*, which can flash in red and green like a railway signal.

Mating

The act of mating varies greatly from order to order, but in most species of insects the male mounts the back of the female. Sometimes the act of mating is performed during flight; this is typical of dragonflies, craneflies, mayflies, and many wasps, bees and ants. The dance- or bristly-flies of the family Empididae, perform a mating dance and mate on the wing. The male brings his mate a gift of food – some small insect of another species – for her to eat while mating. This may be a precautionary instinct for some females are known to eat their mates during the mating act. The biting midges of the family Ceratopogonidae have predatory females; the female midge seizes a male and sucks out the contents of his body while copulation takes place. The female praying mantis is also liable to eat her mate, and may indeed mate

76

with and devour several males in succession.

Mating processes vary. In some apterygote insects the male produces a droplet of sperms that he transfers to the female in his mouthparts. In other primitive insects the male attaches a stalked spermatophore to the ground and induces the female to walk over it.

Once fertilized, the female lays her eggs. The location in which the eggs are laid is carefully selected to suit the life-style of each kind of insect. Insects that spend their immature lives under water lay their eggs either directly into the water, like the mayflies, or on plants or rocks close to the water so that they can fall in. The water-beetle *Dytiscus* inserts its eggs into the stems and leaves of water plants. There they can mature in safety while having a moist environment.

Blowflies lay their eggs on the carcasses of dead animals, or in the wounds of living ones, so that the larvae will have ample supplies of their normal food when they hatch. Most houseflies lay their eggs in fresh manure. Plant-eaters lay their eggs on

the plants on which the young will later feed. Bees build elaborate nests of wax, and wasps construct theirs of paper, creating individual cells for the eggs. Some insects such as locusts and cockroaches enclose the relatively delicate eggs in a stout outer casing, or capsule, known as an ootheca. Such confined quarters would not be a wise choice for the young of the familiar green lacewing fly. The predatory lacewing larvae are cannibals, and the first one to hatch would probably eat the rest. So the lacewing suspends each egg individually on a thread, attached to a plant infested by greenfly.

Ovipositors

In order to introduce their eggs into the right environment, most females possess an egg-laying organ known as an ovipositor. This is basically a long, tube-like structure which enables the insect to place her eggs precisely where she wishes. The blowfly, for instance, has a long, flexible ovipositor designed for inserting eggs deep into the cracks

75. *Trypoxylon* is known as the organ-pipe wasp because it builds a vertical tube of mud. Starting at the top the wasp divides the nest up into a number of cells by means of mud partitions. One egg is laid in each egg cell, which is then stocked with paralyzed spiders and sealed.

76. Another mud-dauber wasp, *Trigonopsis*, makes two or three horizontal cells stacked one above the other. The wasp lays an egg in each cell as it is completed and then stocks the cell with small cockroach nymphs which are paralyzed. When full of prey the cell is closed with mud. This picture shows the insect's long curved jaws holding a ball of liquid mud.

77

78

79

82

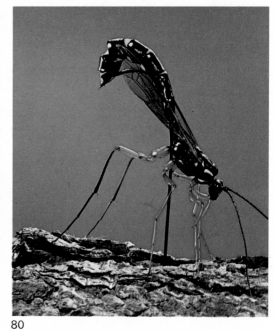

80

and crannies of a dead animal. Grasshoppers have a rigid, drill-like structure which they use to make holes in the soil, laying the eggs out of sight and danger. Many craneflies of the genus *Tipula* use their ovipositors more like a pickaxe than a drill. The female raises her body high in the air on her long, fragile legs, then drops it so that the ovipositor on the end of her abdomen strikes the ground. A deep enough hole may take as long as forty minutes to hack out. Incidentally, this insect provides an example of the confusion that may be caused by popular names. It is often called a daddy-long-legs, a name which is also given to the harvestmen, which are arachnid relatives of the spiders.

The sawfly, a relative of bees and wasps in the order Hymenoptera, takes its name from the shape of its ovipositor, which has teeth like a saw and is used to cut slits in stems and leaves. The sawfly's relative, the wood-wasp, has a drill-like ovipositor which is powerful enough to bore through the bark and into the wood of conifers.

81

83 84

77. *Sceliphron cementarium* is the best known of the New World mud-dauber wasps. The arrangement of cells is similar to *Trigonopsis* but they are stocked with paralyzed spiders. The wasp is about to begin to seal a cell which is fully stocked, as revealed by spider legs sticking out of the entrance.

78. The *Pepsis* wasp is called a tarantula hawk because it seeks out large tarantula spiders that live in the ground. The wasp tempts the spider to leave its burrow and then quickly paralyzes it with well-directed stings. The prey is dragged down the tunnel which is filled in after *Pepsis* has laid her egg.

79. The wood-wasp *Urocerus gigas*, which is frequently mistaken for a large wasp, has no sting and is harmless. The ovipositor consists of three stylets that interlock to form a tough hollow drill which deposits the eggs inside the wood of coniferous trees.

80. The *Rhyssa persuasoria* female drills down to reach a full-grown wood-wasp larva or pupa which is within two inches of the surface of the wood. The ovipositor, which is in three parts, is inside the protective sheaths.

81. With great precision the ovipositor enters the wood-wasp tunnel, stings the larva or pupa to paralyze it and then deposits an egg on the host.

82. Female pupa of *Urocerus gigas*. The wood-wasp larva spends two years burrowing in timber; when full-grown it bores towards the surface and pupates at a depth of approximately $\frac{3}{4}$ inch. The young adult escapes by chewing an exit tunnel.

83. In the warmer parts of the world dung beetles do a very useful job in distributing and burying animal waste. Each beetle collects a ball of dung and rolls it away backwards before burying it.

84. *Necrophorus vespillo* is a burying beetle which excavates beneath a small dead vertebrate until it comes to lie underground in a chamber. Several eggs are then laid in adjacent cells.

85

86

87

The larvae may take up to three years to develop, by which time the wood may have been cut down, sawn into planks, and used for building. The European wood-wasp, *Urocerus gigas*, which is black and yellow, is often mistaken for a hornet. It is common in pine forests and deposits its eggs in this way. But the wood-wasp is itself the victim of another Hymenopteran, the parasitic ichneumon, *Rhyssa persuasoria*. *Rhyssa* is more than one inch long and has an ovipositor of twice that length. Having used its antennae to detect the host larva as it tunnels its way through the tree, *Rhyssa* drills down to where the wood-wasp grub is at work and injects a paralyzing fluid. It then lays one egg next to the larva. In the same way the North American wood-wasps, or horntails, of the genus *Tremex*, which bore into hardwood trees, fall victim to ichneumons of the genus *Thalessa*. The latter have giant ovipositors, up to six inches long. It is not known for certain how the ichneumon wasps detect their prey. It cannot be that the parasite responds to movement, since an immobile pupa will also be accurately located in the wood. Smell is the most likely sense to be involved.

Preparation for egg-laying

Many of the beetles work hard to make provision for their young. Dung beetles, as their name implies, feed on the excrement of other animals, generally that of mammals. They form a family of about 300 species, the Geotrupidae. Most members of the family dig deep tunnels into easily-worked soil. As usual, it is the females that do the work, but often the males help by removing the soil thrown up by their tunneling mates. A tunnel may be up to seventy inches deep, with short horizontal galleries leading off it. Each gallery constitutes a brood chamber, in which one egg will be laid. The parent gathers a ball of dung and stuffs it into each gallery to provide food for the newly-hatched larva. Some of these shafts are dug in free ground, but generally they are located close to a manure heap, sometimes directly below it.

The scarab beetles, sacred to the Ancient Egyptians, are also known as pill rollers from their habit of making a ball of dung, which the female rolls along the ground. As it moves the ball may grow from the size of a walnut to bigger than a tennis ball. Eventually the beetle digs a burrow and buries the ball of dung inside it, sometimes as much as eleven inches below the surface of the ground. The beetle remodels the ball of dung as an egg-chamber, cementing one egg inside it.

Many families of beetles feed entirely on vegetable matter, and the females strive to prepare suitable breeding grounds for their young. Some leaf beetles of the family Chrysomelidae gnaw holes in tree branches and there lay their eggs. They seal up the holes with lids of dung held together with a cement secreted by the female. Such beetles prefer the living wood for their eggs; others need dead or decaying wood, and make their egg chambers in fallen trees. A genus of long-horn beetles, *Onicideres* (Cerambycidae), actually produce their own dead wood for their larvae. The female chews a deep notch around a small living stem or tree branch which kills that part of the tree above the damage. The beetle then lays her eggs in holes in

88

89

90

85–90. *Danaus plexippus*, the monarch butterfly of North America. A pair are mating on milkweed, their food plant (85). The monarch is a strong flier and accomplished glider. Each year in autumn the butterflies migrate a distance of approximately two thousand miles south from Canada and the northern United States to Florida, Mexico and California, where they congregate in vast numbers on certain trees to winter-over. In spring they begin their flight north, laying their eggs on the milkweed plant, *Asclepias*, along the way (86), and finally dying. The ribbed and fluted eggs are laid singly and hatch in a few days (87). The caterpillars exhibit typical warning coloration (88). They eat the leaves and succulent stems of the milkweed, so called because the sap is white and viscous, although very poisonous to most animals. The caterpillars absorb the poison without ill effect, but if a bird eats the caterpillar it at once vomits and presents an appearance of great discomfort. One experience is sufficient to teach a bird to leave monarch larvae alone. The full-grown caterpillar hangs head-down and molts into a beautiful green pupa ornamented with flecks of gold (89). The pupa gradually darkens until just before emergence the color of the adult wings can be clearly seen (90).

the bark beyond this point. In a strong wind, the weakened tree or branch falls to the ground and the larvae continue their tunneling and complete their development in the dead material provided by their mother.

It is notable that insects which go to great lengths to make provision for their young generally lay only up to a hundred eggs. By contrast stick insects, which leave more to chance, lay many thousands of eggs, so that even though most perish, enough survive to carry on the species.

Eggs come in a great variety of shapes and sizes: cylindrical, spherical, long, thread-like, some the size of pinheads, others so small they cannot be seen clearly with the naked eye. But they all have certain features in common. Each egg contains sufficient yolk to nourish the tiny embryo; each has a protective toughened shell; and each needs a supply of oxygen and water if it is to develop. Eggs of many species of insects can remain dormant if kept dry. An .example is the South African locust, *Locustana pardalina*, whose eggs have been kept in a desiccated state for three and a half years, yet have hatched once moisture was available.

Many insects go to great trouble to ensure their eggs will have sufficient moisture. The eggs of whiteflies, hemipterans of the family Aleyrodidae, are laid on the leaves of plants such as cabbages. Each egg has a kind of stalk, which is inserted into the leaf in such a way that the egg stands up like a peg. Through the stalk the egg absorbs moisture from the plant. If the leaf shrivels, the eggs do not develop.

Egg development

The eggs take in moisture through a modified region of the outer casing, known as the hydropyle. Eggs may double in size through the absorption of moisture; but once sufficient moisture is acquired the eggs cease to take it in.

The shell of an insect's egg is called the chorion. If the eggs are to be exposed to the elements, like those of butterflies, the chorion is relatively thick,

91–4. Emergence of monarch butterfly. When ready to emerge the butterfly ruptures the pupal cuticle along the back of the thorax by pushing hard against it. Slowly the insect withdraws its legs and antennae as it works its body forward (91). When the legs are free the butterfly reaches up, grasps the pupal case and withdraws the abdomen; it is completely formed except for the wings (92), whose complete expansion is rapidly achieved (93) by the influx of blood from the body into the wings. There will be an interval of several hours however before the wings are fully hardened and the insect can fly. The empty pupa is somewhat unusual in being completely transparent and it will remain hanging until dislodged by wind or rain. The striking pattern of the monarch (94) is easily recognized by predators, but the butterfly frequents open country where it flies and glides without attempt at concealment. This is because the toxins taken in by the caterpillar are transmitted through the pupal stage into the body of the adult, and one monarch contains sufficient poison to kill a small-to-medium-size bird if the insect is not expelled in time. For this reason the monarch is mimicked by a number of edible, unprotected butterflies of other families.

91

92

93

94

with a layer of wax on the inside which is deposited by the embryo itself. The wax ensures that the egg is waterproof, except at the hydropyle. Often there are also porous regions or channels which allow oxygen to permeate from the outer air, or from water if the egg is laid in a stream or pond. There is also, in the majority of insect eggs, one or more ducts known as micropyles which allow sperm from the male to fertilize the egg before it is laid. With some insects, fertilization takes place before the shell is formed.

Some eggs are covered by only a thin chorion; examples are locusts, water-beetles, and some of the parasitic Hymenoptera. The chorion of locust eggs often breaks up; the embryo makes good the loss by secreting a cuticle containing chitin and protein around itself.

Although in the normal way eggs hatch when conditions are suitable, development may also stop even in favorable conditions. This is a state known as diapause. Often the diapause is induced by a drop in temperature, and then the egg enters a period of hibernation; an example is the wintering-over of the fertilized eggs of aphids, mentioned on page 106. In very dry weather aestivation, a summer dormant state similar to hibernation, takes place; then a rise in humidity may be enough to set the growth mechanism working again.

Most insects lay several hundred eggs; for example, the housefly lays two or three batches of about a hundred eggs each. However, these numbers seem small when compared with the egg output of the social insects. A queen honey bee lives up to five years, and spends most of that time laying eggs. An estimate of the quantity produced in a lifetime is around 1,500,000. A queen termite of the species *Macrotermes natalensis* can lay about 30,000 eggs a day, and lives for ten years – the total egg production during her life must be staggering. This may well not be the record, since a queen of the species *Odontotermes obesus* has been observed to lay 86,400 eggs in just one day! However, queen termites do not necessarily lay every day, but produce eggs according to the

95

96

97

requirements of the nest.

The amount of post-natal care provided by insects is generally minimal; having laid the eggs in the most favorable situation, the mother has no further interest in them, and indeed may well be dead within a few days, long before the eggs are hatched. But there are exceptions; for example in some Hemiptera and, also, notably the social insects – bees, wasps, ants, termites – there is an elaborate system for caring for the young, which is described in Chapter 6. Solitary bees and wasps also have an interest in the young that extends beyond the egg stage.

Parental care

Wasps of the genus *Bembix* leave the cells containing the larvae unsealed and bring each larva food every day, carefully concealing the tunnel entrance after each visit. The female wasp makes her nest underground in sandy soil, usually near those of other wasps of the same species. A colony of fifty nests is not uncommon. The nest may con-

tain half a dozen larvae, each of which will require up to eighty flies on which to feed during the fifteen days it is a larva. *Bembix* captures its victims on flowers or in flight. The American cicada killer, *Sphecius speciosus*, on the other hand, lays in stores beforehand. The female digs a burrow with a number of side passages. In each side passage she stores a cicada, which has been stung and paralyzed. The wasp then lays her eggs on the cicadas. When the eggs hatch the larvae feed on their paralyzed but still living victims. The cicada killer attacks cicadas on the wing and then drags the paralyzed bodies to its burrow. If dragging the food home is too difficult the wasp will airlift the cicada. However, since the combined weight of wasp and cicada is too heavy for ordinary take-off, the cicada killer laboriously climbs a tree with her victim, and so gains enough height for the flight back to base.

Many species of beetles and true bugs also take care of their young after they have hatched. The female shield bug, *Elasmucha griseus*, lays its eggs

95–7. *Agraulis vanillae* – the gulf fritillary. The caterpillar (95) feeds on the passion flower, *Passiflora* sp., and although Central and South American in origin this butterfly is easy to rear on the correct food plant in greenhouses in temperate countries. The caterpillar is well protected by stiff spines (96) which dissuade predators such as birds. But spines are no protection against insect parasites such as ichneumon wasps. The adult (97) is noteworthy for having most beautiful silver blotches on the undersurface of the hind wing. It is a common garden species in Trinidad, where it is called the silver-spotted flambeau.

98

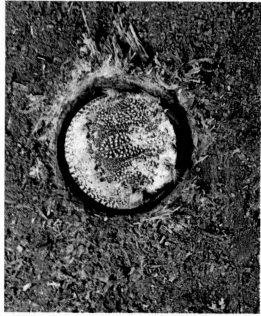

99

100

101

98–104. *Pantophthalmus tabaninus*, one of the world's largest flies. In Trinidad members of OSF found holes up to ½ inch diameter in a large log and piles of wood fragments on the ground below. This was a challenge to investigate. After much labor with saw and axe an enormous grub was found at a depth of 7 inches, living in an open tunnel (98). The small dark head is armed with a pair of powerful jaws, as one would expect in a woodborer. The rear end of the larva terminates in an armored plate which fits the tunnel fairly tightly and presumably serves to exclude predators (99). The plate may perhaps also serve as a shovel to eject wood fragments. The presence of a

on a leaf and then crouches over them, shielding them with her own body. She also guards the young nymphs the same way. In some species of giant water-bugs, Belostomatidae, the female cements her eggs to the back of the male, who is left to carry the babies until they hatch. He then rests at the surface and dips his body as each egg hatches so that the young can slide into the water.

Some of the leaf beetles show parental care. The female poplar beetle, *Phytodecta rufipes*, remains on guard over the young until the third molt. Some scarab beetles stay close to their eggs until the young have not only hatched but have matured. Here the brood is small, consisting of around four eggs.

A different form of caring for the young is shown by the burying beetles of the genus *Necrophorus*. These beetles find the bodies of small animals such as birds, moles or mice and bury them in the soil – usually to a depth of only a few inches, though some graves may be as deep as twenty-four inches. Several beetles, males and

females, share the task of burying, but when the work is done the strongest female chases off all except one male. She lays her eggs close to the corpse on which she feeds until the eggs hatch. The grubs feed first of all on a partly predigested food, chyme, which the female regurgitates, and then on the carrion.

Metamorphosis

The pre-adult life of insects is a fascinating one, and with few exceptions is by far the longer part of their life. During this period the insect goes through several changes, some of them dramatic. The process is known as metamorphosis, and there are basically two kinds: complete and incomplete. With complete metamorphosis, the insect passes through four stages in its life; with incomplete metamorphosis there are three.

Complete metamorphosis is undergone by insects of the nine orders which make up the Endopterygota – that is, butterflies and moths, true flies, alder, snake and lace-wing flies, scorpion

102

103

104

flies, caddis flies, fleas, bees, wasps, ants, and saw-flies, beetles and the parasitic stylopids. Even among the insects of this group the process of metamorphosis varies. The simplest way to understand it is to consider the metamorphosis of the butterflies and moths, and then look at the variations.

The insect when it first hatches from the egg is totally unlike an adult butterfly. It is in the form of the familiar caterpillar, a cylindrical, often hairy creature with up to sixteen legs. The legs which are additional to the insect's normal six thoracic legs are known as prolegs, and they occur on the third, fourth, fifth, sixth and tenth segments of the caterpillar's abdomen. In some species one or more pairs of prolegs are missing, and a few caterpillars have no legs at all.

Caterpillar development

Caterpillars come in a large variety of colorful shapes and sizes but the color of the caterpillar bears little relation to the coloring of the adult. For example, the grayling butterfly *Hipparchia semele* is gray-brown with yellowish patches; its caterpillar is a sulphurous yellow. The purple emperor, *Apatura iris*, is vividly marked in purple, brown and white; the caterpillar is a sleek, banded green shot with yellow. The chalkhill blue, *Lysandra coridon*, is largely blue as its name implies, while its caterpillar is green and yellow. The coloring and marking of caterpillars are largely related to their environment (see Chapter 5).

The caterpillar spends several weeks feeding and growing. It usually begins by eating the shell of its own egg and then moves on to other food, mostly vegetable. At this stage it consists of thirteen body segments, of which the first three form the thorax and the rest the abdomen. It has a large head with powerful mouthparts adapted for chewing. Close to its jaws are two short antennae, and below the mouth is a spinneret, an organ that exudes a secretion which hardens at once to become a silken thread. The silk helps to give the caterpillar a foothold, particularly during molting.

Like an adult insect, the caterpillar has an exoskeleton which does not grow. In order to have room for growth the caterpillar must therefore change its skin. This periodic molting normally occurs four or five times during the caterpillar's life. Under the old skin is a new one, which initially is soft and elastic enough to allow the caterpillar to grow. Growth is therefore a series of steps, rather than a gradual progression.

When the caterpillar has completed feeding after the last of its molts it is ready for the final stage in its pre-adult life in which it casts its skin and emerges as a pupa or chrysalis. This is a quiescent stage when the insect cannot feed. Having selected a suitable place to form itself into a pupa the caterpillar prepares for the great change. Different species of Lepidoptera have their own methods; some spin a complete silken cocoon in which to pupate; others construct cases made of bits of leaf, held together with silken strands; still others pupate with no protection, relying on camouflage to avoid predators. Many moths make cocoons, but butterflies do not. The

pair of large spiracles at the posterior end shows that the grub must belong to the order Diptera (101). In front of the spiracles are gills which presumably function when the tunnel becomes waterlogged; certainly the timber in which OSF found the larvae was always very wet. The pupa (100) is extremely active and can move backwards and forwards along the tunnel. When the adult fly is ready to hatch the pupa sticks the head end out of the tunnel before the pupal case splits open (102). The insect thus emerges without hindrance (103). The adult female is up to almost an inch in length and of thickset build (104).

45

105

106

107

108

109

majority of butterfly caterpillars attach a blob of silk to a suitable leaf or twig, and hang from this by hooks on the abdomen while they change into the chrysalis. Blood pressure splits the caterpillar's skin behind the head and it is worked back down the body by waves of expansion and contraction. At first the newly-formed chrysalis is very soft, but it quickly hardens and assumes its final shape, in which the future appendages of the adult can be distinguished. During development of the adult inside the chrysalis a complete reorganization of the body tissues takes place. At the moment of pupation some adult features already exist, but the formation of the rest is carried out by the remaining body tissues breaking down into their basic materials and reforming. This process may take as little as ten days, but the adult insect does not always emerge so quickly. The chrysalis provides a suitable form in which the insect can winter-over, waiting until the temperature and other conditions are favorable for adult life. In cold-winter climates, therefore, the chrysalis

105–11. *Culex pipiens*, the common gnat. This is one of the most abundant European species of mosquito. It breeds in close proximity to man in garden ponds and water barrels – in fact in any small body of water existing for the few weeks it takes for the life cycle to be completed. 200 or more conical eggs are laid together in the form of a raft which is concave above and convex below (105). The larvae hatch from the lower part of the egg directly into the water; they are very active and progress by a jerky doubling and straightening of the body. Breathing depends on atmospheric air, which is taken into the body through a siphon by which the larva suspends itself at the water surface (106). Brushes of hairs are used to sweep tiny particles into the mouth. The pupae are easy to distinguish from the larvae (107), although they too are very active, diving down at the first sign of danger by powerful thrusts of the tail paddles. The pupae breathe through a pair of trumpets on the thorax. Before the adult fly emerges the pupa stretches out horizontally at the water surface; the thorax splits open mid-dorsally and the mosquito emerges into the air without getting wet (108). The relatively simple antennae show that this is a female: many long hairs arise from the antennae of the male. Gradually, the appendages, wings and abdomen are worked out of the pupal sheath (109, 110) until the fly rests momentarily on the water surface to harden before flying away (111). Female mosquitoes must suck blood before their eggs mature.

110

111

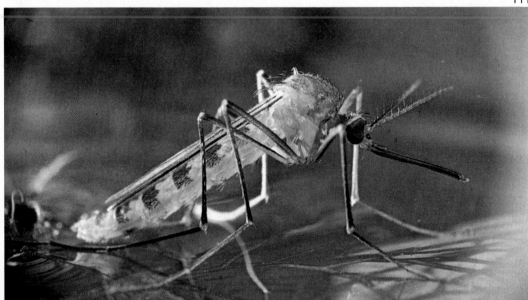

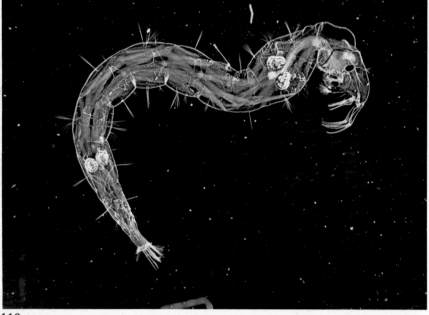

112

113

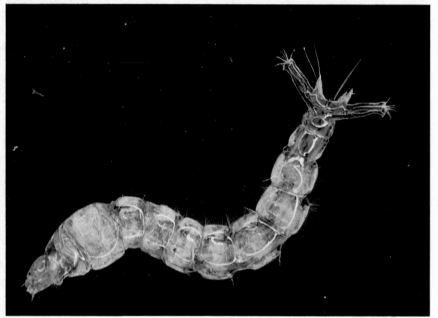

114

115

116

112. The larva of *Chaoborus crystallinus* known as the ghost or phantom larva. At the front and hind end are a pair of air-sacs which function as hydrostatic organs that enable the insect to float at any depth.

113. The numerous filaments on the head of a pupa of *Chironomus* absorb oxygen from the water and enable the pupa to remain at the bottom. There is a well developed tracheal system which fills with air by the time the adult is ready to emerge so that the pupa floats to the surface.

114. The larva of the midge *Tanypus* lives under water but breathes through a pair of respiratory trumpets at the end of the abdomen.

may remain in existence for several months. Temperature is apparently the controlling factor in some cases, but in others glandular secretions inside the insect determine the length of pupation.

In the final stage, the thorax of the newly-formed adult swells to crack open the chrysalis. The insect pulls its legs free, and uses them to drag the rest of its body out of the pupal skin. At this stage the wings are wet and crumpled, and the exoskeleton is still soft. The young butterfly hangs wings down, from a twig or leaf while blood is pumped through the veins of the wings to swell them to their proper shape and size. Meanwhile the exoskeleton hardens and the butterfly's legs become firm. The adult is generally ready for flight within an hour or so, but the hardening process sometimes takes much longer.

The metamorphosis of houseflies from egg to adult is very similar to that of butterflies and moths. The larvae, known as maggots, are legless, moving about by wriggling or squirming. In most species of flies the last larval skin acts as a sort of cocoon inside which the insect pupates.

Many flies, such as mosquitoes and midges, have very active aquatic larvae and in some of these species the pupae are unusual in that they are active too.

Cocoon-spinners

Several kinds of insects spin cocoons for the pupal stage. The most familiar example is the cultivated silkworm moth, *Bombyx mori*, from which all our silk comes. Ants also form cocoons, and these are the familiar so-called 'ant eggs' sold as fish food. Adults which have biting mouthparts escape from the cocoon by chewing their way out. Some wild silk moths (Saturniidae) have a special tooth at the base of each fore wing by which they tear the silk apart. Another method of escape used by certain Saturniids is to plaster the inside of the cocoon with a secretion which softens silk; they then push their way out.

All the other insects with wings (the Exopterygota) and the wingless insects (the Apterygota) go through an incomplete metamorphosis. Indeed, the Apterygota generally go through so small a change from the time they hatch until they are fully grown that they can hardly be said to undergo a metamorphosis at all.

Incomplete metamorphosis

Again, it is easiest to follow the process with one particular order of insects, such as the dragonflies and damselflies of the order Odonata. In describing the process, entomologists use the term 'instar' to describe the stage between any two molts. The final instar, or adult form, is called the imago. As the insect emerges from the egg it is in an immature form called a pronymph; this stage lasts only a matter of minutes, and this instar then sheds its first skin to emerge in the second stage, as a nymph. Dragonflies hatch under water, and the larger part of the nymph's life is aquatic, the nymph breathing through gills, like a fish. The number of instars varies from ten to fifteen, the insect growing larger at each molt but not changing much in shape, apart from the increase in size of the wing pads.

This period of development lasts from one to five years, according to species. A little while before development is complete the nymph stops feeding, just as a caterpillar does before pupating. The gills cease to function, and the nymph emerges from the water so that its spiracles can begin to absorb oxygen from the air. It stays like this for a while, during which time the remaining internal changes take place. Then during the hours of darkness, the nymph climbs up some suitable object such as the stem of a plant, and grasps it firmly with its claws. After a while the exoskeleton splits open along the back of the thorax, and the head and upper part of the body of the adult insect emerge. Gradually the insect pulls the rest of its body clear, leaving the old exoskeleton still clinging firmly to the plant.

The adult insect generally hangs from this nymphal skin while the wings are expanded and the cuticle hardens. By daylight it is ready to take to the wing.

Most other insects in the Exopterygota have a

117

life cycle similar to that of the dragonflies, but of course only some develop under water, and those which pass all their lives on land have no gills.

Insect caste system

The development of exopterygote insects in which there is a caste system is somewhat more complicated. Termites have four castes; workers, soldiers, and the reproductive kings and queens. The instar at which the final caste of the adult insect becomes apparent varies from species to species. In some, the differences are obvious from the second instar; in others, they may not show up until the sixth or seventh instar.

Among the most simple developments are those of the biting and sucking lice, which form the orders Mallophaga and Anoplura. They appear to have only three instars, and develop to adult life in between twelve and twenty days. In the true bugs (Hemiptera) the number of instars varies between species from three to nine; five or six is the usual number. The bugs go through consider-

115. The curious larva of *Microdon* was first described as a new genus of land Mollusca! In fact it is a hoverfly.

116. These spangle galls of the gall wasp *Neuroterus quercusbaccarum* produce a unisexual generation of wingless females whose eggs give rise to round currant-like galls from which males and females emerge.

117–24. *Schistocerca gregaria*, the desert locust. This insect causes much damage in North Africa and is probably the species responsible for the plagues of Egypt quoted in the Book of Exodus. During mating the smaller male sits on the back of the female who may continue crawling and feeding.

118. Breeding by locusts takes place in sandhills with sparse vegetation. The female drills a hole with the tip of her abdomen vertically down into the sand and extends her pliable abdomen so that the eggs are laid about 4 inches below the surface. About 50 eggs are laid and as the female withdraws her abdomen she fills the tunnel with a white secretion which forms a firm plug (119). Development of the eggs is continuous and the time taken to hatch depends on temperature. At 75°F the eggs will hatch on the twenty-first day. These eggs are 19 days old and the eyes of the embryo can be seen through the cuticle (120). The locust hatches as a vermiform larva: the whole insect is enclosed in a thin transparent membrane which probably protects the larva as it works its way to the surface. As soon as the larva emerges from the soil it sheds the cuticle and resembles an adult in general appearance (121). The term 'hopper' is used for this and the succeeding four instars. The first instar hopper is dark when fully hardened (122). At first the head is abnormally large, but as it feeds the abdomen increases in size, while the head does not.

The 4th instar hopper has obvious wing buds which in fact first appear in the 3rd instar. Changes in body pattern and coloration have also occurred (123). The 5th instar is the pre-adult stage, and after feeding for several days the hopper climbs a plant and hangs head downwards. Air is swallowed to distend the abdomen, the wing buds are forced apart and the cuticle splits on the thorax. Aided by gravity the adult emerges fully formed except that the wings have yet to expand (124).

118

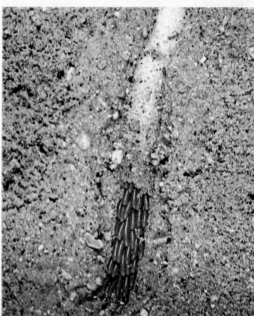

119

120

121

122

able changes from one instar to the next, and particularly from the last nymphal stage to the adult.

The wingless insects of the Apterygota also pass through a number of instars, but basically the first instar is much the same as the adult in all but size. The silverfish, *Lepisma saccharina*, is a good example of this. The firebrat, *Thermobia domestica*, molts every twelve days or so, and becomes adult at about the twelfth molt. Thereafter it continues molting at intervals throughout its long life. But in no pterygote insect is the adult ever seen to molt.

Viviparous insects

A surprisingly large number of insects complete the process of embryonic development inside the body of the parent, and emerge as living young, instead of as eggs. This process is known as viviparity. This characteristic is most common among aphids, strepsipterans and some flies. The exact course of development varies from one

123

124

species to another. Blowflies and houseflies may retain their eggs so that hatching occurs as the eggs are laid. In the fleshfly, *Sarcophaga carnaria*, the eggs hatch within the female, who gives birth to larvae.

These and similar examples among the Diptera all rely on the yolk of the egg for the nourishment of the embryo. But the female tsetse fly (*Glossina*) not only hatches the eggs inside her body, but nourishes the larvae until they are fully grown. Only one larva is produced at a time; it feeds from a small nipple within the uterus and molts several times. Pupation occurs immediately after birth. Tsetse flies produce only about a dozen young during their lives, an unusually slow rate of reproduction in the insect world.

Another group of flies which produces young one at a time, ready to pupate, is the Pupipara. These are curious ectoparasites, either wingless or with reduced wings, that live on the blood of birds and mammals. Some of the tiny flies known as gall midges, Cecidomyiidae, also produce living young.

125-31. *Ficidina viridis*, emergence of a cicada. Cicadas are common in the warmer parts of the world and more than one thousand species have been described. The nymphs live underground where they suck sap from the roots of trees and shrubs. The developmental period in the soil is always long, usually four or five years, but *Magicicada septendecim* of North America holds the record at seventeen years. At the end of the growth period the nymph claws its way out of the soil and ascends a convenient tree to a height of several feet (125). This is the nymph of *Ficidina viridis*, a common cicada in Trinidad. Having found a suitable place the nymph takes up a vertical position, head up, and grasps the bark firmly with the claws. Soon blood is pumped into the thorax — the greenish tinge of the blood is just visible — and the nymphal skin ruptures in the mid-dorsal line. At once the head and thorax of the adult bulge out of the slit (126), the legs and tiny wings quickly follow so that the insect projects horizontally from the nymphal skin (127). The white strands are the cuticular linings of the anterior spiracles. The cicada next reaches up and grasps the pupal skin while the abdomen is withdrawn. The wings begin to expand as blood is pumped into them (128).

Expansion of the wings progresses rapidly (129, 130) and within ten minutes the wings are full-size (131). There is now a resting period of several hours while the insect hardens. Cicada nymphs usually emerge from the soil under cover of darkness. By the time the sun is up the following morning the adults are able to fly and sing, but after years spent hidden underground the cicada lives to sing in the sunshine for only two or three weeks.

125

126

127

128

As described on page 33, many aphids are viviparous at the time when they are producing young without mating. The two characteristics often go together. The aphids breed so fast in this stage of their annual cycle that the young as they are born already have embryos of the next generation maturing inside them. This reproduction by immature insects is known as paedogenesis. It occurs in some gall midges, and also in a primitive beetle, *Micromalthus debilis*. This is the only beetle whose larvae are capable of reproduction.

The larvae of insects are as varied in form as the eggs from which they hatch and the adults into which they ultimately change. The shape of larvae is conditioned by the kind of life they lead and the type of food they eat. Some, such as the larvae of butterflies and moths, need to move freely about plants, which they consume at a great rate. These are the so-called polypod or many-footed larvae, such as the familiar caterpillars and fast-moving, caterpillar-like larvae of the sawflies and scorpionflies. They have extra prolegs on some of

their abdominal segments.

The active, predatory larvae of many beetles, neuropterans and trichopterans have only the typical six legs on the thorax with none on the abdomen. They are known as 'oligopod,' meaning 'few-footed.'

The larvae of a great many insects are apodous – literally, having no legs, and indeed few appendages of any kind on the body. The maggots of the true flies (Diptera) are all legless; they move about by squirming, and generally do not have to move far to find food. Many parasitic insects have larvae of this type, particularly those whose larvae live within the host's body.

Similarly, the legless grubs of furniture beetles – the so-called woodworms – and other larvae that bore through timber need no legs. The larvae move by gripping the tunnels they make by expanding the segments at the head end. Then the hind end of the body is pulled forward, the front segments relax and are extended and the process is repeated. What such larvae do need, and have,

129

130

131

are powerful jaws and mouthparts which enable them to bite and chew their food.

Gall-makers

One final aspect of the lives of miniature insects to be considered is the relationship with plant galls, knobby excrescences which are formed on many plants. Galls have a variety of causes, including the action of bacteria, viruses, molds, mites and roundworms. But a great many are caused by insects, for whom they provide a home during the development stage. Gall-making insects are found among the beetles, moths, aphids, thrips, flies and wasps.

The most important of the gall-makers are the gall wasps, which form the superfamily Cynipoidea. Most gall wasps are very small, and difficult to spot and identify. One of the most typical galls is the oak apple, an irregular, ball-shaped growth which is found on oak trees. It is caused by *Biorrhiza pallida* which lays its eggs in the soft green buds near the end of the young oak shoots. The insect

does not form the gall itself but in some way not fully understood the plant is induced to grow abnormally. If you cut open an oak apple you will find a number of cells inside, each of which provides a home for a grub.

Biorrhiza pallida is one of many gall wasps that have a very complex life history; two quite different generations are produced during the year. The wasps that eat their way out of the oak apple are of both sexes. After mating in July, the female crawls down the trunk and enters the soil where she seeks out small roots. Eggs are inserted into the root tissue and the resulting galls are small spheres about three-eighths of an inch in diameter. During winter the root galls produce wingless females which make their way up to the soil surface and ascend the oak trunks. Those which survive the weather and escape attack by hungry birds lay their eggs in the terminal buds. During the following May the oak apple galls begin to swell and with the appearance of the bisexual generation the life cycle is complete.

Chapter 4

Food, Senses and Flight

As with most members of the animal kingdom in their natural state, the activity of an insect can be summed up in two words: feeding and breeding. All their actions, including flight and migration, are directed to one or both of these two ends.

As we have seen, many insects do not feed in their adult life, but merely mate, lay eggs, and die. However, all insects eat in their immature stages. They eat almost anything organic, that is, living or having lived. Some insects chew their way through fresh green leaves, others prefer the desiccated and seemingly inedible contents of museum showcases. Some eat flesh, others plants, and still others carrion. Some eat solid foods, others suck up liquids. Insects may be divided into four groups: herbivores, which eat plants, carnivores, which eat other animals, omnivores, which eat both; and scavengers, which eat decaying matter.

The study of fossilized remains of prehistoric insects suggests that there have been both carnivores and herbivores from very ancient times. The fossils include many insects whose living descendants, such as cockroaches, mayflies, dragonflies and silverfish are very similar. It seems likely that the general habits of these prehistoric insects were similar to those of their descendants. From this we would expect the early mayflies to have been vegetarians, like today's mayfly nymphs, and the ancestors of modern dragonflies to have been carnivores like their descendants. Some modern cockroaches are omnivores, others vegetarians, and their ancestors may well have been the same. What does seem probable is that prehistoric insects enjoyed a more catholic diet than present-day ones. In the overcrowded conditions of the earth today insects have developed specialized features that enable them to feed on one particular type of food. When the world was younger the range of food available was probably more restricted, and insects may well have needed a more varied diet in order to survive at all.

All food comes originally from plant life. Even the carnivores depend on that, because they eat creatures that eat plants. For that reason, you will always find most insects where and when there is an abundance of rich green vegetation: along river banks, for example, and in the spring growing time. In this way, a chain is formed: carnivores eat plant-eaters which eat plants. These food chains, as they are called, are very important in the study

133

132. When at rest, with its wings closed, the emperor butterfly (*Morpho peleides*) is inconspicuous in the dappled light of the forest. This somber coloring of the undersurface of the wings contrasts strongly with the iridescent blue of the upper surface (see pl. 165).

133. Tiger beetles (Cicindelidae) are very active predators and fly readily if disturbed. Many species are brightly colored but this species, which lives on beaches along the south-eastern seaboard of the United States, is camouflaged to match its background.

of ecology, the relationship of plants and animals with each other and with their environment. In most environments, the food chains, or webs, have many interconnecting strands.

The herbivores come close to the bottom of the food chain. The vast majority of insects are plant-eaters, and the largest number of the plant-eaters eat leaves. A few insects eat almost any part of almost any kind of plant. Such an insect is the army worm, so called because it appears in vast numbers. The army worm is the caterpillar of *Pseudaletia unipuncta*, one of the night-flying moths, in the family Noctuidae. This green and yellow caterpillar forms marching columns of up to twelve feet long and three inches wide. They eat most of the green matter in their path, hunting by night and hiding by day. Other herbivores with a wide variety of tastes in food include a number of destructive grasshoppers and crickets.

Most other herbivores are specialist feeders: that is, they prefer to eat a few types of plants, and often only one. A familiar example is the caterpillar of the cabbage white butterfly, *Pieris brassicae*, which devours the leaves of cabbages and similar plants, and also those of nasturtiums. Less familiar but equally typical are the water-dwelling mayfly nymphs, which scrape minute

134

135

136

137

134. The larvae of the cabbage white butterfly (*Pieris brassicae*) feed voraciously for about twenty days before pupation. During this period they molt four times, growing markedly with each change of skin.

135. The larvae of green lacewings (Chrysopidae) feed upon aphids, using the empty husks of previous meals as camouflage. In this picture an aphid can be seen clasped in the larva's powerful mandibles.

136. This larva of the gulf fritillary (*Agraulis vanillae*) is busy feeding on the leaves of the passion flower. The great majority of caterpillars feed upon the leaves of green plants and have powerful jaws.

plants called algae and diatoms off rocks. Incidentally, it is these plants which make so many underwater rocks slippery.

Many plant-eaters restrict themselves not only to certain plants, but to particular parts of those plants. For example, the caterpillars of the silkworm moth, *Bombyx mori*, eat the leaves of one particular species of mulberry tree, *Morus multicaulis*. The larvae of the asparagus beetle, *Crioceris asparagi*, browse only on the stems of asparagus. Among the smallest vegetarians with specialized tastes are the leaf-miners. These minute larvae tunnel between the upper and lower surfaces of leaves which may then curl over as a result. Some species complete their development within the thickness of the leaf; others grow too large and end up by feeding on the outside, often protected by a case made from leaf fragments. Leaf-miners are mostly the caterpillars of tiny moths, but some are the larvae of beetles and flies.

Another group of specialized plant-feeders is the juice suckers, which use mouthparts shaped

somewhat like miniature hypodermic needles to suck the sap of plants. Most of the true bugs belong to this group, among them the familiar greenfly, blackfly and other aphids, and the scale insects, which include the cochineal insect. Many aphids and scale insects produce a substance called honeydew. This is a clear liquid in which sugar in excess of the insect's requirements has become concentrated. It is eagerly sought after by ants, bees, and many species of flies. The plant suckers not only damage the plants on which they feed, but they also spread disease among plants.

Anthophilous (literally, 'flower-loving') insects are another specialized category of vegetarians. They include all the insects which feed on the nectar or pollen of flowers, such as wasps, bees and many species of butterflies, moths, beetles and true flies. It is interesting to note that it is the adult forms which feed on pollen and nectar. This is because such feeders need wings in order to move from one plant to another. Thus the diet changes with the development of the insect; the leaf-eating caterpillar turns into the nectar-eating moth or butterfly.

Some insects devote their attentions not to the stalks or leaves of plants but to their roots or seeds. The root-eaters are mostly beetle and fly larvae, though some of the gall wasps also attack roots. Probably the best known root-feeder is that long, slender creature, the wireworm, which is not a worm but the larva of beetles belonging to the family Elateridae. The wireworm's normal food consists of the roots of weeds and grasses, and it ravages crops that are sown on newly-plowed grassland. Another familiar creature in the soil is the leatherjacket, which is the larva of a crane-fly (Tipulidae). Some moth caterpillars also feed on roots, especially those of swift moths (Hepialidae). The root-feeders are pests not only in agriculture but also in nurseries.

Other insects misnamed worms are those found in flour and cereal grains of all kinds. The best known are the larvae of beetles of the family Curculionidae, commonly known as weevils. There are a great many species, each of which has its own food preference. They are generally known by the name of the plant whose fruit or grain they attack, such as the nut weevil *Curculio nucum*; the water-plantain weevil *Hydronomus alismatis*; and the grain weevil *Sitophilus granarius*, which can play havoc in granaries.

Many insects prefer a harder diet and feed on the bark or wood of trees. The furniture beetle, *Anobium punctatum*, generally called woodworm, is the best known of these insects. The beetles lay their eggs in cracks or crevices. When the larvae hatch they bore into the timber, in which they make extensive, destructive tunnels. In the forests where they live naturally they perform a useful function by helping to break up fallen trees and reduce them to a condition in which they will decay. They and their close relative the death-watch beetle, *Xestobium rufovillosum*, feed on timber that has long been dead. Incidentally, the sinister-sounding tapping of the deathwatch beetle is produced not by the larva which is chewing the timber, but by the adult beetle. It is a mating call. Another relative is the powder-post beetle, *Lyctus*, which prefers to eat recently-dead sapwood, the outer starch-filled layer of a tree which surrounds the heartwood. Many termites also eat timber. Engraver beetles eat the layer of living tissue between the bark and the timber of trees; this layer is known as the cambium.

Carnivorous insects

The carnivores are a mixed group feeding on living flesh, blood and carrion. Some carnivores eat any part or all of their prey; others specialize in one kind of food, even from one kind of animal.

Predators are the hunters among the insects. The beautiful, delicate-looking dragonflies are typical predators. They eat anything they can catch, both as adults and while they live in the water as nymphs. As they grow, they work their way gradually up the size scale. As very young nymphs they feed on protozoa, the one-celled animals. During the five years which some spend as nymphs they eat small crustaceans and when fully grown they have a diet of tadpoles and tiny

138

fish. The adult dragonflies are poor walkers, so they catch all their prey on the wing. These are other insects and even other, smaller dragonflies.

At ground level the predators include a wide variety of beetles in the family Carabidae, the ground beetles. Many of them cannot fly, and they hunt on foot by night, preying on other insects and such animals as earthworms. Both larvae and adults follow much the same life-style and habits. Closely related to the ground beetles are the tiger beetles (Cicindelidae), which have earned their common name because they are among the fiercest and most predatory of all insects. They have strong, large mandibles for seizing their prey. The larvae dig themselves burrows and wait unseen for any small insect such as an ant to pass within range. One swift movement, and the beetle larva has seized its quarry, which it eats in the depths of its burrow. The adult tiger beetles are swift runners and fliers, and can easily overtake their victims.

The dragonflies are not the only insects that

137. The larvae of scarab beetles usually take several years to grow because they live among rotting plant debris and in dead wood which are not particularly nutritious. This individual was found in a rotting log in Jamaica.

138. The Hemiptera or true bugs all have characteristic mouthparts adapted for sucking. Although some species feed on blood, the great majority live on plant juices like this coreid nymph.

139

140

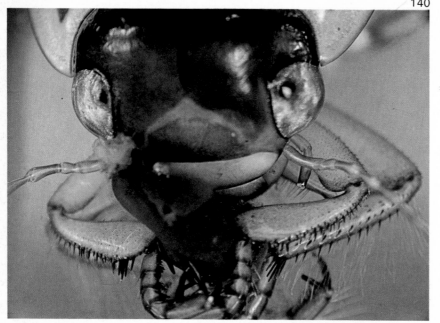

appear too fragile to be hunters. Lacewings, slow and delicate fliers, eat quantities of aphids, both as larvae and as adults. By contrast the robber flies of the family Asilidae look as they sound: strong and vigorous, with a horny proboscis used to stab and paralyze the victim. In size they are medium to large, but their appetite and aggression are enormous and they frequently attack other flies and insects such as grasshoppers which are as big as themselves or bigger. Another group of predators is the hoverflies (Syrphidae). In the larval stages these insects eat large quantities of aphids, but when adults they turn vegetarian and drink nectar. Incidentally, it is just as well that aphids breed and multiply so rapidly, since they form the staple diet of many other creatures, including ladybugs.

The blood-suckers form a very large group among the carnivores, and include such flies as mosquitoes and midges. The bite of a mosquito is actually the prick of the insect's needle-like proboscis that drives into the skin to suck the blood. A minute tube in the proboscis allows saliva to flow

141

142

143

139–40. Giant waterbeetles of the genus *Dytiscus* are predatory both as larvae (139) and as adults (140). Any creature in the right size range will be attacked. In these pictures the victims are tadpoles.

141–2. Dragonfly larvae (*Aeshna* sp.) are also aggressive predators and like waterbeetle larvae, will attack animals much larger than themselves. After creeping slowly within range (141) the prey is seized by the 'mask.' This is the labium, modified into a huge claw hinged beneath the head. After capture (142) the victim, here a water louse (*Asellus*), is drawn to the mouth.

143. Adult dragonflies, like the larvae, are also predatory. In this picture, taken in a swamp in Georgia, the dragonfly on the right has just captured another dragonfly on the wing and has alighted to feed.

into the wound, causing the itching that follows a mosquito attack. However, the only mosquitoes that suck blood are the females; the mouthparts of the males cannot puncture skin, so the males are of necessity vegetarians. The females, too, drink plant juices as a large part of their diet, and it would seem that they drink blood to acquire certain chemicals they need for the development of their eggs. Some mosquitoes attack only birds; others feed exclusively on the blood of man. They are major disease-carriers (see Chapter 7).

Parasites

Most of the parasites can be grouped with the carnivores, since they feed on the blood or other body fluids of their hosts. There are two kinds of parasites. Ectoparasites, such as fleas and lice, live on the outside of the hosts. These insects are really predators, but they are too small to kill their prey and merely cause it some inconvenience. Endoparasites live all or part of their lives inside the body of a host, whose death they may cause.

Flesh flies are a kind of endoparasite because they lay their eggs in wounded or infected parts of their hosts' bodies. They include blowflies and screw-worm flies. Botflies and warble flies lay their eggs on the outside of the host animal's body, and the grubs make their way inside by various means. The ox warble fly, *Hypoderma bovis*, has a typical life history. The adult warble fly lays its eggs on the hairs of cattle. When the larvae hatch they bore their way into the skin, and spend some months inside the animal's body, finally making their way to just below the skin on the back. There they pierce small holes so that they can obtain oxygen from the air. At this stage a small swelling, the warble, forms on the animal's back. The larvae inside each warble feeds there until it is fully grown, when it wriggles out of the hole and falls to the ground to pupate.

The horse botfly, *Gasterophilus intestinalis*, also lays its eggs on the hairs of its host, generally a horse, mule or donkey. But the larvae rely on fastening to the horse's lips when the animal is

144

144. The praying mantis
(Dictyoptera) is perhaps the
most familiar of all predatory
insects. Here *Stegomantis
limbata* from the
south-western United States
is feeding on a moth.

145. These Trinidadian ants
were observed on a freshly
grown bracket fungus
striking at fungus gnats
(Mycetophilidae) and trying
to capture them on the wing
as they flew in to lay their
eggs.

grooming itself, and thus enter the horse's digestive system. They are carried to the stomach,
where they attach themselves to the lining and
feed. When they are ready to pupate they let go
and pass out of the body with the dung.

A large number of endoparasites prey on other
insects, and most of them belong to two orders,
the Diptera, true flies, and the Hymenoptera. Such
parasites are mostly very small indeed. Among the
smallest are the fairy flies, in the hymenopteran
family Mymaridae, and those in the genus *Alaptus*
are the smallest of the lot. *Alaptus psocidivorous*,
found on the Pacific Coast of North America, is
about eight hundredths of an inch long in the
adult stage. It lays an egg in the egg of the ten-
spotted psocid, *Peripsocus californicus*, a small
booklouse which lives on trees, and is itself only a
few hundredths of an inch long.

Other endoparasites lay their eggs on larvae,
pupae or adult insects. The parasite larvae feed on
the blood and fat of their hosts, thus ensuring that
no vital organ is attacked and that the host will

145

146

147

148

146. Parasitism is a common phenomenon among insects, particularly in the Hymenoptera. The larvae of the braconid wasp *Apanteles glomeratus* are parasitic in the caterpillars of the cabbage white butterfly, *Pieris brassicae*. In this picture the larvae have emerged and are pupating in yellow silk cocoons beside the body of their host.

147. The minute wasp *Aphidius metricariae* is another braconid. Here it is attacking the aphid *Myzus persicae* in which the larvae will develop. This wasp is bred for the biological control of aphids in hot houses.

148. This cuckoo wasp (Chrysididae) is a parasite of mud-dauber wasps (*Sceliphron* sp.) in Arizona. Other chrysidids parasitize potter wasps (*Eumenes*) and the solitary leaf-cutting megachilid bees, some of whom are also parasitic themselves.

continue to live and provide room and board. Many parasites bore their way out of the body of the host in order to pupate, but some pupate inside. Then the final stages of the parasite's immature form generally kill the host, which by this time has served its purpose.

Parasites themselves are not immune from the attacks of parasites. The poet Jonathan Swift, writing in 1733, commented:

So, naturalists observe, a flea
Has smaller fleas that on him prey;
And these have smaller fleas to bite 'em,
And so proceed *ad infinitum*.

Allowing for a certain amount of poetic license, Swift was right, and the process, known as hyperparasitism, can go several stages. The peach aphis, *Myzus persicae*, may be attacked by four species of parasites, minute wasp-like creatures. Three of these parasites are themselves the victims of hyperparasites: *Aphidius phorodontis* is liable to attack by three species of Charipinae, most of whose relatives are gall wasps.

Finally, there are the omnivores, insects which like both flesh and vegetation. They include the housefly, the cockroach, many wasps and some crickets. Sometimes the scavengers, carnivores and herbivores which eat dead or decaying matter, are also placed in a separate category. Among their numbers are many insects which are regarded as pests, because they eat materials of economic importance, such as the wool of carpets, cooked meat, or the timber of furniture. Beetles and flies form a very large part of the scavenger group. In nature, they do a very important job, helping to ensure the rapid disintegration of dead matter so that its basic chemical components become available for the next stage of the general cycle of life.

The feeding habits of insects show very clearly the many ecological niches they fill – that is, their part in the general life of the community of living things. This topic is discussed more fully in Chapter 7. To carry out their varied roles insects have very highly developed senses, which are directly related to the special type of life they lead.

149

150

149. In this view of the mantid *Stegomantis limbata* the well developed compound eyes are clearly visible. Note also the chewing mouthparts and their associated palpi.

150. The harlequin beetle, *Acrocinus longimanus*, is the largest and most striking of Trinidad's Cerambycidae. The antennae are each about five inches long. The compound eyes are unusually large for a beetle and the mandibles can deliver a painful bite, easily drawing blood.

Almost all insects can see, though the quality of vision varies greatly. A worker ant, for example has very poor vision, and can probably do little more than tell light from dark. A dragonfly, on the other hand, which hunts by sight, can see small objects up to forty feet away.

We saw in Chapter 1 that insects have two kinds of eyes: compound and simple. Each compound eye consists of a number of facets, each of which is a tiny light-focusing lens. The number of facets varies enormously. Workers of the ant species *Solenopsis fugax* have in each eye nine or fewer facets. On the other hand the queens have 200 and the males 400. The worker ants spend most of their lives underground and have little need of vision, whereas the other classes of ants go into the open and fly. The male ants, which need to locate the females, have the best sight.

That is one end of the scale. At the other, dragonflies have up to 28,000 facets to each eye, which accounts for their greatly superior vision. In between these two extremes come insects such as the housefly, which has about 4,000 facets to each eye, and butterflies which have between 2,000 and 17,000 according to species.

Vision

What sort of sight do these compound eyes provide for the insect? Nobody really knows. It is generally thought that the many lenses, which are called ommatidia, build up a mosaic-like picture in the brain of the insect. As each lens has a visual range of between 20° and 30° there must be considerable overlap between neighboring lenses, but a network of inhibitory nerve fibers in the eye prevents the signals from adjacent ommatidia becoming superimposed and confused. Obviously, the sight mechanism inside an insect brain is extremely complex although the brain itself is smaller than a pin head. Bees and wasps have particularly good eyesight. Digger wasps in the family Sphecidae supply their nests with flies for the young larvae to eat. They never catch anything but flies, and they can even distinguish between hoverflies and wasps, which hoverflies closely resemble. Birds are deceived by the hoverfly's disguise; the digger wasp is not. It catches hoverflies freely, never taking a wasp by mistake.

The most interesting visual sense so far studied in detail is the color sense of the honey bee. After many years of patient experiments the German zoologist Karl von Frisch discovered that bees have a well-developed color sense; they cannot see the panorama of different shades that humans can, but they can distinguish six colors. Moreover, bees do not see the same colors as we do. A bee cannot see red, which has the longest wavelength of the colors we see; but it can see ultraviolet, which is invisible to us. The bees' color range consists of ultraviolet, bluish-green, violet, Bees' purple (which is a combination of ultraviolet and yellow), yellow and blue. Most insects appear to be red-blind, with the exception of butterflies. For this reason many clear red flowers are not pollinated by bees, but are visited by butterflies. Many brilliant red flowers in Africa and America are pollinated by birds, which can see red.

A bee's many-faceted eyes also help it to navigate. Its brain can measure the angle at which the sun strikes the eye, and so determine in which direction it is flying. If the sun is obscured by cloud its position may still be detected by analyzing the plane of polarization of light from the sky. This navigational technique is also used by various other insects. The bee can also calculate its ground speed while flying, since an object seen by one facet or group of facets will be picked up by another group a split second later. The bee's brain is programmed to measure this difference. The bee can also measure its air speed by noting the degree its antennae are bent as it flies. With all this information it can calculate the exact course back to the hive.

Bees are not the only insects which have built-in windspeed indicators. Many other flying insects have them; butterflies and blowflies, for example, will not take off if the speed of the wind is too strong for them to fly against it. The insects rely on scent from flowers and other food sources being wafted to them by the wind, and they must then fly up-wind to reach their goal.

As we have seen, bees have a complex built-in navigational system. But many other insects also have this ability. Locusts, for example, appear to navigate by detecting the earth's magnetic field, effectively having built-in magnetic compasses.

Migration flights

With the aid of these senses, many insects navigate considerable distances when migrating. Such migrations are not the outcome of chance winds, but are controlled flights with a set objective. The zoologist C. B. Williams once saw three different streams of migrating insects flying over the Masai plains in Tanzania at the same time. Some large yellow butterflies, *Catopsilia florella*, were heading north-north-east; a swarm of small yellow butterflies, *Terias senegalensis*, flew south-west; while millions of locusts, *Schistocerca gregaria*, headed south-east. The three traffic streams mingled in apparent confusion about nine feet or less above the ground – but there were no collisions, and the fliers were not thrown off course by the rival migrants.

Many migration flights are sparked off by over-population. This is particularly true of locusts, Acrididae, which from time to time form dense swarms and fly off into the blue. Many of these mass flights end with the death of most of the swarm. The same thing happens with many species of butterflies and moths. Hawk moths from tropical Africa fly north over the Mediterranean Sea to southern Europe, and some have been seen as far north as Iceland; cabbage white butterflies from the Baltic Sea area migrate westwards over the North Sea to the British Isles.

But in addition to these periodic flights, which resemble the mass exodus of lemmings, zoologists have found a number of regular migration patterns, particularly among butterflies. The best-known migration is by the monarch butterfly of North America, *Danaus plexippus*. During the summer months monarchs are seen in the Hudson Bay area of Canada. During the fall they fly south and west to winter-over in the southern states and Mexico. Those that get as far south as Mexico breed there, but those wintering further north, in California, Florida and Louisiana, hibernate in large swarms, roosting in trees. The butterflies always use the same trees, and in some places, such as Pacific Grove, California, the butterfly roosts are a tourist attraction, protected by law.

By marking individual butterflies, entomologists have proved that some complete the round trip, returning to Canada in the spring accompanied by many others which have bred either in Mexico or during the journey north.

This south-in-autumn, north-in-spring migration pattern is also found with a number of other species of butterflies and moths, both in North America and Europe. These insects include the red admiral, *Vanessa atalanta*, the small tortoise-shell, *Aglais urticae*, and the large cabbage white, *Pieris brassicae*. The painted lady, *Vanessa cardui* breeds in southern Europe and northern Africa, but some individuals migrate northwards every year to places such as the British Isles and Iceland where the climate is too inhospitable for them to

151

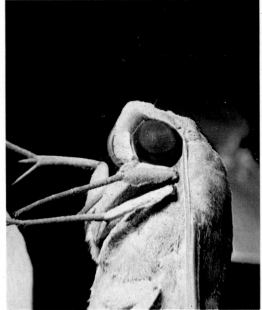

152

153

151. Head of the European house cricket *Acheta domestica* (Gryllidae) showing the compound eye.

152. The compound eye and the body, densely clothed in scales, can both be seen in this picture of the Jamaican hawk moth (Sphingidae) *Pholas nutuphon.*

153. In this picture of the Trinidadian butterfly *Opsiphanes* sp. (Brassolidae) the long proboscis used for sucking nectar from flowers is partly uncoiled. The sense organs that cause the proboscis to be straightened are in the butterfly's front feet.

154

155

154, 155. Among the true flies (Diptera) the development of the compound eyes is often remarkable, virtually enclosing the entire head. Such eyes are particularly sensitive to movement and are associated with a high degree of flight control. The antennae, although small, are nevertheless well endowed with sense organs.

156, 157. Ant lions (Myrmeleontidae) belong to the order Neuroptera, which includes the lacewings and alderflies. Superficially they resemble dragonflies but the clubbed antennae immediately serve to distinguish them. The larvae usually live at the bottom of conical pits excavated in dry dusty soil.

winter-over, even in hibernation.

Other senses

Man himself is responsible for some local migration. By rotating crops he moves the preferred food of many species of insects from one place to another; but the insects always catch up with the crops, sometimes arriving in swarms.

As we have seen, the sense of smell is important in finding food and in finding a mate; the sense of sight is important in finding food and in travel. But insects, as a class, also possess three other senses, those of hearing, smell and touch.

Sounds are used by many insects, such as the cicadas and the crickets, during courtship. But sounds may also be recognition signals, and it is believed that bees, in particular, identify other members of the same species by the engine note of their beating wings. For other insects the wing-beat notes of predators may act as a warning.

Many insects are hunted by bats, those remarkable flying mammals that hunt with a kind of

156

157

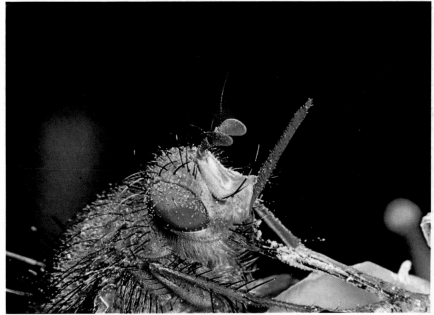

158

sonar. The bat emits a series of ultrasonic bleeps and locates its prey by the echo of the bleeps, which it picks up with its large, sensitive ears. To catch noisy insects such as flies and mosquitoes, the bat does not even need to switch on its sonar – it can home in on the sound of the wing beats. However, much of the bat's hunting is done at night, and the main quarry then is the night-flying moths. Moths make no sound as they fly, so the bat has to use its sonar to locate them. If silence were the moths' only protection, few would escape the bat; but the moths themselves are equipped with sensitive hearing organs which can pick up the bat's ultrasonic bleeps. As soon as they hear the bat coming the moths take evasive action, diving, looping, and swerving like combat aircraft in a dogfight. Some just fold their wings, shut off power and drop like stones.

Scientists investigating the moth v. bat war detected ultrasonic sounds coming from some of the moths. These sounds are apparently a warning that the moths in question have an unpleasant taste, and therefore serve the same purpose as, for example, the warning colors displayed by day-flying insects such as wasps.

One sense that is highly developed among all insects is that of touch, or feeling. The hard suit of armor which encases an insect's body prevents it from having the same all-over sense of touch as the human body. But its body is covered with little sense organs, sensilla, consisting of tiny slits, hairs or bristles which are linked to the insect's nervous system. Sensilla are particularly numerous on the feet and legs, and on the antennae, which are the main sense organs.

Most insects use their antennae in various ways. These highly sensitive organs can detect movements in the air, including certain sound waves. They are used to touch objects, and in this way to identify and measure them. In most antennae there are also well-developed organs of smell and taste; indeed, the borderline between touch and taste appears to be finely drawn in many insects. Antennae also record vibrations: this can clearly be seen in the busy antics of whirligig beetles

159

158. In this view of the Tachinid fly *Adejeania vexatrix* the small but nevertheless complex antennae typical of the Diptera are clearly seen.

159. *Climaciella brunnea* (Mantispidae) is a neuropteran that, as an adult, is predatory. The mantid-like raptorial front legs are used to seize prey. This species is unusual in being a wasp mimic.

160. The characteristic clubbed antennae of the butterflies are clearly seen in this head on view of the Trinidadian nymphalid *Callicore aurelia*.

161. Saturniid moths are among the largest Lepidoptera in the world. The pectinate antennae are extremely well developed, particularly in the males, as may be seen in this Indian moon moth, *Actias selene*. These specialized antennae are used to detect minute traces of scent emitted by the female to attract a mate. Male moths will assemble to a female from several miles away.

160

161

162

163

162. Many Orthoptera possess very long antennae. This immature pterochrozine tettigonid has antennae that are four times longer than its body.

163. The longicorn beetles (Cerambycidae) are well named for they, too, often possess very long antennae. The benefits to be derived from such structures are not clear and might well be thought to create problems when flying.

(Gyrinidae), which skim about on the surface of ponds and sluggish streams. Each beetle keeps its antennae lightly touching the surface of the water, and can thereby detect the movements of other insects, especially those on which it feeds.

Insects also use their tactile sense for measuring. Caddis worms, the larvae of caddis flies, Trichoptera, make cases for protection by combining silk which they spin themselves with grains of sand, bits of shell and other materials. Each case is just long enough to contain the caddis worm, and the larva measures the case for size with sensory hairs at the tip of its tail. As the case is being constructed, the larva carefully measures each stone before slotting it into place, rejecting those of the wrong size or shape. Bees measure the cells they make and take immediate action to correct them if they are the wrong size. Queen bees check these cell measurements before they lay their eggs. This is because large cells are for drones and small ones for workers. The queen fertilizes the worker eggs, but not the drone eggs.

Flight development in insects

Only three groups of animals possess the ability to fly under their own power: bats, birds, and the majority of insects. A few other animals such as flying squirrels, flying phalangers, and flying fish can glide, once launched into the air, and many kinds of spider balloon by means of silk parachutes. But these creatures have no real control over the speed, direction or duration of their flight.

Insects are the oldest of the flying animals; their wings evolved about 300 million years ago. These wings originated in a way quite unlike those of bats and birds. The wing of a bat or a bird is the modified front leg of a four-legged animal. The wing of an insect is a quite separate projection from the body.

Insect wings appear to have developed from paddle-like outgrowths, called paranota, which grew on the sides of the three segments which form the thorax. Some zoologists believe that when some prehistoric insects took to jumping,

164

165

as grasshoppers and fleas do today, they used these paranota as fixed wings to help them glide in the same way as a flying squirrel today uses the flaps of skin on either side of its body.

Insects remarkably similar to today's dragonflies are among the earliest fossil insects with wings, so the dragonfly's wing system may be considered as possibly the nearest to the prototype. Some early fossils show that all three segments of the thorax had paranota, though it would seem that only on the two rear sections, the mesothorax and metathorax, did the paranota develop into the wings we know today. There was never a six-winged insect as far as we can tell.

Mechanism of flight

Dragonflies can hover or fly backwards or forwards at speed, but they do not have the versatility of flight of many bees and flies. This also suggests that their flight mechanism is at a relatively early stage of development. Their wing beats are slow when compared with those of bees, and particularly with those of many species of flies.

The wing of an insect consists of a double layer of exoskeletal material containing chitin. Each layer is so thin that most wings are transparent. The wings are stiffened by corrugation and by fine hollow horny rods, called veins. Along these veins run tracheae, nerves, and sometimes a blood supply as well. The venation (vein pattern) is superficially similar in all insects, but the subtle variations help entomologists to identify and classify different families, genera and species.

The structure of insect wings and the virtually indestructible substances of which they are made ensure that they will survive long after most of the insect has disintegrated. For this reason fossil impressions of wings are frequently found in rocks, clearly showing the venation. This helps enormously in the classification of prehistoric insects and in tracing the probable course of flight evolution.

The number and size of the operational wings of insects vary. Dragonflies, for instance, have two pairs of wings of almost identical size. But with

166

most other kinds of insects, though they have two pairs of wings, the size of the two pairs varies. In many insects these two pairs of wings can be worked independently, but it would appear that the most efficient flight is obtained either by one pair of wings – as with the true flies, Diptera – or by co-ordinating the work of the two pairs so that they operate effectively as a single pair.

Wasps, bees and ants have a row of hooks, called hamuli, along the leading edges of their hind wings. These hooks fit into the trailing edges of the front wings, which are turned under to form a continuous groove. Thus locked together, the two pairs of wings beat as one. Butterflies and many moths have a huge overlap of the fore wings and the rear wings, which also ensures that the two work together.

Dipteran flies have developed the front wings for flight. The rear wings have become reduced to halteres, slender stalks terminating in a knob. These halteres are sensory in function and help the flies to keep their balance in flight.

164. Scales removed from the wing of a butterfly.

165. The emperor butterfly *Morpho peleides* and its close relatives in the family Morphidae are among the most striking inhabitants of the forests of the tropical Americas. The iridescent scales on the upper wing surfaces catch the eye as the butterflies flit through the trees.

166. The small postman *Heliconius erato* is a widespread and abundant butterfly in Trinidad, where it inhabits the lower forests. At night this species gathers, often in considerable numbers, at selected roosting sites. This picture shows the start of such an assemblage.

167

168

Beetles use their rear wings for flight, and the fore wings have become transformed into leathery wing-cases, called elytra, which protect the flying wings while the insects are on the ground. Grasshoppers and their relatives in the Orthoptera have leathery front wings, while the true bugs have wings known as hemelytra, which are leathery near the root and membranous at the ends.

Insect flight differs from that of birds and bats in that the wings themselves have no muscles. Instead, they are powered by a double set of muscles inside the thorax. In the simpler forms of wing action, such as that of the dragonfly, the muscles act directly on the wing roots.

In flies and other insects with very quick wing movements, it is the structure of the thorax which makes such movement possible. The material of which the thorax is made contains the protein resilin, one of the most elastic substances known. A ball made of it would go on bouncing for ages. The muscles actuating a fly's wings are called indirect muscles, because they act on the thorax and not directly on the wings. One set, running vertically inside the thorax, pulls the top of the thorax down. The wings are hinged in such a way that this downward movement of the thorax makes the wings go upwards, much as pulling on the handles of a pair of oars makes the blades move the opposite way.

Then the second set of muscles comes into play. These muscles run horizontally along the length of the thorax. As they contract, the top of the thorax springs back into shape, and the wings are depressed.

In higher insects the wings often beat at very high frequencies – up to 1,000 beats a second in some midges. No nervous system is capable of transmitting impulses at this speed. In these insects the flight muscles have a characteristic fibrillar structure and the ability to self-generate a cycle of contraction if suitably loaded. The wing beats in such insects are largely a matter of automatic oscillation, governed by the mechanical resonance of the combined thorax and wing system once initiated by a single nervous impulse. Generally speaking, the smaller the insect the higher the frequency of wing beat, and your ears will confirm this as you listen to the 200 beats per second droning of a bee's wings against the 500 or more beats per second of a mosquito.

All the nerves have to do is to start the vibration off; self-generated booster impulses keep it going. The nerve impulses for change of speed and direction control different sets of muscles from those used for moving the wings up and down. These are not fibrillar but require a nerve impulse for each contraction.

There is one further ingredient in high-speed insect flight. The wings themselves are in effect spring-loaded, like an electric light switch which snaps over to make or break contact, no matter how fast or slowly you move the lever controlling it. This device, known as the click mechanism, consists of tiny catches which hold the wings in either the up or the down position, until there is sufficient tension in the muscles to trip them and send the wing flashing from one position to the other. The click mechanism helps to increase the speed of movement very considerably.

Insect aerodynamics

There is a popular belief that, according to the laws of flight as understood in conventional aviation, an insect such as the bumblebee should not be able to take off because its body is both heavy and bulky in relation to its wing size. But in fact insect wings are subject to the same laws of aerodynamics.

A wing provides lifting power because of the way in which the air flows around it. An airplane wing section, called an airfoil, has a rounded leading edge, and is thicker at the front than at the back, where it tapers away to nothing. In addition, the under-surface is slightly concave and the upper surface is convex. This shape of wing causes the air flowing over it to move faster and farther over the top surface than it does under the lower surface. The result is an actual lifting force, or suction, applied to the wing from above. If the front edge of the wing is raised at an angle to the

169

170

flow of the air over the wing, the lift is increased – up to a certain point. With airplanes, an angle of 15° or more produces a condition known as stalling; there is insufficient lift, and the aircraft drops like a stone. With insects the angle can be very much steeper, up to 60° in some species, before stalling takes place.

Obviously, insect wings are much more complex than those of airplanes for they do not just move up and down, but twist and flex in flight, effectively altering the airfoil section during the course of each stroke. An insect steers by twisting its wings, and this movement is performed by additional sets of muscles which adjust the angle at which the wing is hinged to the thorax. Such adjustment, being carried out by different muscles, is completely independent of the continuing vibration of the wings themselves.

The reason the bumblebee is able to defy, apparently, the laws of aerodynamics is a complex one. For one thing, the very speed of wing movement – about 200 times a second for a bumblebee –

167, 168. The front pair of wings is modified in beetles to form a pair of tough, rigid elytra. At rest (168) the elytra of the weevil *Phyllobius* cover and protect the membranous hind wings. In flight (167) the hind wings unfold to provide a large propulsive area. The elytra are thought to provide lift in a manner similar to the fixed wings of conventional aircraft.

169. The palm weevil *Rhina barbirostris* shown here is just about to take off. Note how the elytra are folded forward to enable the hind wings to unfold and provide the power.

170. The wings of many flying insects beat at a very high frequency. In order to provide the necessary power the flight muscles need to operate at a temperature several degrees above that of the rest of the body. This picture shows a shield bug (Pentatomidae) vibrating its wings in pre-flight warming-up exercises.

171. The soldier beetle *Chauliognathus leconti* (Cantharidae) occurs in the mountains of south-eastern Arizona. It is seen here on take off.

172. A metallic green bee of the genus *Euglossa* hovering by the freshly opened flower of the orchid *Gongora*. The bees are attracted by a special scent emitted by the orchid, which relies on this particular species for its pollination.

173. Mayflies (Ephemeroptera) are a rather primitive order. Most of their lives are spent under water, where they may live for two or three years. The adult life is very short, often lasting less than one day. Mayflies are unusual in having a winged subimago, which subsequently molts into the adult. Mayflies often emerge at sundown in astronomical numbers at certain seasons. This swarm, seen against the setting sun, was photographed in Florida.

171

172

173

creates greater power and, owing to the ever-changing wing configuration, greater lift.

The very smallest of insects, the fairy flies, of the order Hymenoptera, are so small that for them the air is quite a viscous substance. The air has about the same resistance as water has to a large animal, and flying is more like swimming. Fairy flies, which are minute parasitic wasps in the family Mymaridae, are quite tiny, with a wingspan of four hundredths of an inch. Their wings are shaped like oars and are covered in bristles.

Insects fly much more slowly than most people imagine, though in relation to their size the speeds are prodigious – comparable with those of model trains, which travel at scale speeds much faster than their full-sized counterparts. The fastest authenticated speed flown by an insect was that of a dragonfly, *Anax parthenope*, which reached a speed of eighteen miles per hour over a short distance. *Tabanus bovinus*, a species of horsefly, has been timed at more than eight miles per hour. Another fast flier is the convolvulus hawkmoth,

Herse convolvuli, but since these moths fly only at night, observations have so far been unable to confirm that they are as fast as *Tabanus*. Most bees and butterflies appear to travel at speeds of between six and ten miles per hour. Incidentally, the larger butterflies such as *Morpho* are among the few insects that practise true gliding flight. *Morpho*, with its huge wingspan, can float for long distances with an occasional lazy flap of the wings.

Many observations have shown apparent speeds much higher than those just mentioned, but such speeds are probably aided by air currents, such as those which sweep moths and butterflies on long migratory flights over the sea. It is noticeable that the greenbottle fly, *Lucilia sericata*, tests wind speed with its antennae before take-off. If the wind speed is above about five miles per hour, which is faster than the insect can fly, it remains grounded; especially at mating time, when the males need to fly into the wind to pick up the scent of females.

Of the many species of insects which do not

174

possess wings only the Apterygota – the bristle-tails, springtails, and proturans – appear to have a completely wingless ancestry. All the others are wingless modifications of insects which originally had the power of flight but have lost it because their ways of life do not require this ability. They include the fleas and lice, which are parasites, and some other parasites such as the bee louse, *Braula coeca*, and the sheep ked, *Melophagus ovinus*, both of which, despite their popular names, are species of true flies. Many insects that live underground, including such beetles as the red-legged weevil, *Otiorrhynchus clavipes*, and the violet ground beetle, *Carabus violaceus*, are also wingless. Among the ants the female workers and soldiers are wingless, but queens and males fly.

In some species the males always have wings but the females do not. They include the familiar glow-worm, *Lampyris noctiluca*. Some moths have females with either useless wings or no wings at all. They include the pale brindled beauty, *Phigalia pilosaria*, wingless, and the spring usher,

Erannis leucophaeria, almost wingless.

It is by no means certain why the females have lost their ability to fly. One theory is that they are active in cold, blustery weather, and consequently if they had wings they might be blown away from the bushes on which they live and feed. But this theory does not hold for all wingless species; some are active in warm, settled weather.

Wing-beat frequencies

Insect	Beats per second
Butterflies	8–12
Locusts	18–20
Dragonflies	20–30
Large moths	50–70
Bees	190–200
Houseflies	200
Fruit-flies	250
Mosquitoes	up to 600
Midges	up to 1,000

174. Many insects regularly migrate great distances. The painted lady *Vanessa cardui* occurs in many parts of the world and can cover hundreds of miles. The individuals caught in Europe breed in North Africa while those taken in Canada and the United States migrate from Mexico. There are also migrations of this species in Southern Africa and in Australia, some specimens surviving the 1300-mile journey to New Zealand.

Chapter 5

Defense and Concealment

Insects form a major part of the diet of an amazingly large number of other creatures – mammals, birds, amphibians, reptiles, spiders, and even other insects. Like Ishmael, they find every hand against them. The numbers of insects eaten every year are truly staggering: it has been conservatively calculated that even in a smallish country like Great Britain the spiders eat a weight of insects equal to the weight of the human population every year. That figure takes no account of the insects eaten by other animals. World-wide, the total eaten annually is almost incalculable.

Insects thus play a vital part in the process known as the balance of nature, the delicately adjusted mechanism that makes sure the earth, or any one section of it, is not overrun by any one species of animal or plant. By pollination, insects help plants to flourish; by eating seeds and foliage, they prevent the plants from growing too freely. In the same way, the predators of insects help to keep matters in balance: too many insects can mean the destruction of certain plant life, while too few can result in famine for other species of predators.

To preserve this balance it is necessary that insects are not too vulnerable to attack. Over millions of years of evolution, insects have acquired various methods of preventing their own destruction. Some, like the aphids, do this by breeding in astronomical numbers, so that even when the predators have had their fill there are plenty left to ensure the survival of the species. Others resort to various methods of defense, escape and concealment to thwart their enemies.

The first line of defense for insects is that hard outer skeleton which encases the bodies of many adults and larvae. Armor-plate makes a meal distinctly indigestible, and by itself this may be enough to deter most would-be predators. Many adult beetles, which have in addition to the exoskeleton hard, inedible wing-cases, formed by the upper wings, can rely on their armor to some extent, though the strong teeth of bats and the beaks of birds of prey such as owls can quickly crush their way through the armor to the soft meat found within. The biting and sucking lice (Mallophaga and Anoplura) have not only tough, leathery skins, but also greatly flattened bodies which can resist crushing. Fleas are similarly equipped, but while a flea's body is flattened from

176

side to side, that of a louse is flattened dorso-ventrally – that is, from top to bottom. Both kinds of insects are therefore resistant to being destroyed by their hosts' scratching.

Insects are more vulnerable in the immature stages of larvae or pupae. Then the exoskeleton may be soft or virtually non-existent. The caterpillars of moths and butterflies are soft-bodied, and because they spend their time on plants, exposed to the gaze of predators, they are particularly vulnerable. However, many of them, such as the tiger moth, *Artica caja*, are covered by protective coats of prickly hairs or spines, which make them repulsive to the birds which would otherwise eat them.

Some caterpillars are spiky rather than hairy, for example the peacock butterfly, *Inachis io*, which is found from Japan to the Western hemisphere. Many caterpillars of this kind have stinging spikes or hairs, which transmit a poison into any creature that comes into contact with them. Birds and other predators quickly learn to avoid poisonous insects of this kind. Larvae of the froghoppers or spittle bug insects (Cercopidae) have soft bodies. They envelop themselves in a frothy substance known as 'spit' which apparently serves as a protective covering, shielding them both from the heat of

175. The mottled pattern of this pale, unnamed species of cricket from Trinidad makes it almost invisible upon the lichen covered bark of the trees it is resting on.

176. This tree hopper (*Membracis* sp.) belongs to a family of Hemiptera that often assumes bizarre forms. In particular the anterior thoracic segment (pronotum) is greatly enlarged and extends back over the abdomen. In both shape and coloring this species resembles a dying leaf with frayed, brownish edges. Note the tracheal tubes, which are clearly visible within the insect's body.

177

178

179

the sun and from some of their predators.

Some larvae with no natural defenses make their own armor. Notable among these are the larvae of caddis flies, living on the bottoms of ponds and streams. They construct tubular cases in which to live, using a basis of silk to which they attach a variety of particles such as twigs, leaves, grains of sand or gravel, tiny shells and seeds. Some of these cases look like rough stone chimneys, others like tall log cabins. At the approach of danger, the larva retreats inside its case.

Methods of repulsion

Many insects rely not on armor but on weapons. The most familiar are the stings of wasps and bees. The solitary wasps use their stings to paralyze their own prey when hunting, and for defense on occasion; but bees and social wasps reserve their stings solely for defense, and very effective they are too. The chemistry of bee and wasp venom is complicated: enzymes in bee venom liberate histamine from the body's cells, and free histamine is one of the causes of the clinical condition known as shock. In wasp venom, histamine is one of the constituents, together with other poisonous substances. Some ants also produce poison when they sting, and the venom of a few species can actually be dangerous to people who are attacked. Many of these ant venoms are not yet fully understood, but the most common species rely on formic acid, which may be injected by sting or, as with the common wood ant, *Formica rufa*, discharged as a spray. Most of these poisons are used for hunting as well as for defense, but the soldier ants of some species appear to use their poison solely as a weapon.

Termite soldiers fight in one of two ways: with a repellent fluid, or with mandibles. The fluid produced by termites of the genus *Coptotermes* is a white liquid which rapidly becomes tacky like a quick-setting glue, entangling the attacker and the defender. But in the genus *Nasutitermes* a similar liquid can be fired a distance of almost an inch, disabling the attacker but not the termite. Termites armed with huge mandibles can seize attackers, such as ants, and hurl them. In some species the mandibles 'flick' like a man snapping his fingers, stunning the intruder.

Many other insects use various forms of chemical warfare. Water-beetles of the family Dytiscidae can produce a nerve poison which they use for stunning prey, or for defense. These water-beetles are not alone among beetles in possessing poisons for offense and defense; ladybugs, for example, have poisonous blood, which oozes out from the knee joints when the insect feigns death on being attacked. Any predator sampling the blood would suffer for it.

The blister beetles of the family Meloidae also have poisonous blood, the poison being one of a number of substances which produce blistering when applied to the human skin. The best known is cantharidine, which comes from a beetle, the so-called Spanish fly, *Lytta vesicatoria*, and from other related species. It is sometimes hopefully but ineffectually used as an aphrodisiac. Although a minute dose can kill a full-grown man, some birds can eat the beetles without apparent harm.

180

181

177. *Phrynatettix
tschivavensis* is a very
cryptic grasshopper
(Acridiidae) that lives in the
gravel deserts of south
eastern Arizona.

178. Many long-horned
grasshoppers (Tettigoniidae)
are a brilliant green color
which makes them well
camouflaged against the
vegetation upon which they
feed. This *Microcentrum*
species lives in the lush
rainforests of the mountains
of northern Trinidad.

179. This Trinidadian
Limacodid moth resembles
the shape and color of the
flowers among which it
rests during the day.

180–1. Dead leaves on
the forest floor provide a
habitat for many insects. To
escape the attention of
predators many otherwise
unprotected species assume
a brown leaf-like appearance.
In these two pictures we see
examples from the tropical
forests of the New World.
Aeschropteryx (180) is a
moth and *Eublaberus* (181)
is a giant cockroach.

Some insects use a form of gas warfare to protect themselves. The bombardier beetles, *Brachinus*, have a store of protective fluids contained in glands at their rear. The glands secrete minute quantities of hydroquinone and hydrogen peroxide into a secondary chamber, where an enzyme, peroxidase, causes the hydroquinone to be oxidized to quinone. Free oxygen is released and there is a tiny explosion. The vapor is expelled from the secondary chamber into the air, accompanied by an audible popping sound. The vapor has a caustic effect. The beetle's artillery is located in its rear segments, and since it can turn them in any direction it has a wide field of fire. Beetles have been known to fire more than twenty times at intervals of only a few seconds.

Another beetle using chemical warfare is the darkling beetle, *Eleodes dentipes*. When threatened, this insect stands on its head and discharges a quininoid spray from the end of its abdomen.

The appropriately named stink bugs are among

several insects in the order Hemiptera which can produce offensive odors to ward off attackers. Stink bugs are in the family Pentatomidae. Some of them can fire their obnoxious fluids for distances up to twelve inches. Although the fluid smells unpleasant it is generally harmless. Even grasshoppers employ chemical warfare, many species producing an unpleasant froth when alarmed.

Closely allied to the idea of poisonous substances for external defense is an unpleasant taste, which makes an insect less than welcome as a meal for a bird or other animal. The monarch butterfly, *Danaus plexippus*, of North America, famous for its migration habits, is notorious to birds for its unpleasant taste, both as an adult and as a caterpillar. Equally unpleasant-tasting is the caterpillar of the cinnabar moth, *Hypocrita jacobaeae*.

Warning coloration
Unpleasant taste is frequently allied to a warning coloration, and a standard combination is

182–5. Although some Lepidoptera (butterflies and moths) are distasteful or possess defensive urticating hairs, most species are palatable and provide a welcome meal for predators. Caterpillars and chrysalises are particularly at risk as they lack the power of rapid movement. Consequently the immature stages of many lepidopteran species are well camouflaged. Although the adult lappet moth (*Gastropacha quercifolia*) is leaf-like, the caterpillar (182) winters-over inconspicuously on a twig of its food plant, which is often a hawthorn bush. Another form of camouflage, which is found both in insects and spiders is the imitation of bird droppings, like the caterpillar of the Jamaican citrus swallowtail butterfly *Papilio thoas* (183). One of the most intensively studied examples of cryptic coloration is that of the peppered moth *Biston betularia*. Normally the moth is pale (184) and is almost invisible on lichen-covered tree trunks. In industrial areas where atmospheric pollution has darkened the trees a dark form of the peppered moth has replaced the normal one (185). This is perhaps the most frequently quoted example of evolution in action.

182

black and yellow, as seen in wasps. The caterpillars of the monarch butterfly and the cinnabar moth are banded in these warning hues. The adult cinnabar moth is also vividly colored with bright red stripes and dots on a dull-colored background and pink hind wings. These warning signs are confirmed by the presence of a high concentration of histamine in the body. The cinnabar moth's relatives the tiger moths – they are all in the family Arctiidae – are also poisonous to eat. The garden tiger moth, *Arctia caja*, contains several highly toxic poisons, concealed in glands on the hind legs. The tiger is brightly colored with orange hind wings and mottled cream and brown fore wings.

Another group of poisonous moths is that of the burnets (Zygaenidae). Burnets fly in day-time, and their wings glow with a metallic sheen, in shades of green or blue and black, marked with bright red. They fly very slowly, and are easy to spot and catch – if any bird fancies them. But birds learn to leave the burnet moths alone, and

small wonder, for their armory of poisons includes prussic acid (hydrogen cyanide), a substance frequently used in killing-bottles.

There are a great many other insects that advertise their presence, secure in the fact that they are not worth eating. The common ladybirds or ladybugs, in the beetle family Coccinellidae, are poisonous as we have seen, and advertise the fact with colorings of black and red or black and yellow. In general, if an insect is brightly colored and conspicuous in its normal surroundings, you may be fairly sure that there is something about it that makes it unfit to eat. Even so, there are always some predators that are unaffected by the taste or the poisonous characters of insects. The cuckoo, for example, feeds on caterpillars that other birds leave strictly alone. However, there are relatively few cuckoos, so the survival of the insect species is not seriously affected.

Camouflage

Insects without the safeguard of being bad to

eat need to take other precautions. Many do so by camouflage. The simplest way of hiding in the open is to look as much like the background as possible. Many night-flying moths are dull-colored, shades of brown and gray predominating. This coloring helps them to remain invisible when they are flying at dusk or in the dark, but it is also of the greatest importance for their daytime life. Many a moth spends the daylight hours clinging, wings out-spread, to the bark of a tree, in full view of any passing bird. But in each case the mottled color-ing of the wings blends in perfectly with the back-ground. Needless to say, the moth's coloring is directly related to the kind of tree on which it habitually rests. Thus a black and white moth can find concealment on the silvery trunk of a birch tree, while a brown moth hides on the bark of an oak. The green marvel, *Agriopodes fallax*, is pale green with a mottled pattern that almost exactly matches the lichens against which it rests.

The patterns are as important as the colors in helping to hide an insect. This disruptive colora-tion, as it is called, helps not only to make an insect more closely resemble a variegated back-ground, but also breaks up the outline of the insect, thus making its presence much harder to detect. This is particularly noticeable with moths and caterpillars, but can also be seen with many grasshoppers, which have pale stripes down their otherwise green bodies. The green is very similar to the blades of grass among which the grass-hopper rests, while the pale stripe is of much the same buff color as the grass stalks, so grass-hoppers are undetectable in their natural habitat.

It is a fact that if an animal's body is the same color all over, then when it is lit from above, as during daylight hours, the lower part will appear darker. It would then show up against the back-ground, because of the shadow cast. For this reason most animals are darker on top than below, and this rule applies to insects as much as to other creatures. It can be seen in reverse in the water-bugs of the family Notonectidae, fierce underwater hunters which swim upside-down, and are therefore commonly known as backswimmers or water-boatmen. These have light backs and dark undersurfaces. Incidentally, they fly the right way up, and if they are put into a tank lit from below they will swim the right way up, too.

Butterflies and moths often have very different markings on the upper and lower surfaces of their wings. Butterflies rest with their wings folded to-gether, upright above their bodies, so the under-side is displayed. For this reason, a great many butterflies have comparatively somber lower sur-faces to their wings compared with the brilliance of the upper surface. Sometimes the coloring of both upper and lower surfaces is striking, as in many of the fritillaries, and in the *Morpho* butter-fly (see plates 132 and 165). Although the dull colors of the underside may seem vivid against the white background of a printed page, imagine it in the tropical rain forest where the butterfly lives, a region of deep shadows and brilliant, moving specks of light where the sun breaks through the canopy of leaves. In such a setting the broken pattern of the under wings provides a perfect camouflage, much needed for an insect

183

184

185

186. As their name implies, stick insects (Phasmida) avoid being eaten because of their twig-like appearance, which is enhanced by their habit of feigning death (thanatosis). *Acanthoclonia paradoxa* is particularly cryptic because of its markings, which resemble lichen.

187, 188. Tree hoppers belonging to the hemipteran family Membracidae achieve their greatest diversity and abundance in the New World tropics. The enlarged pronotum is often elaborated and embellished in most curious ways, as may be seen in these two species from Trinidad. *Sphongophorus guerini* (188) is an agile flier despite its shape. The function of the bulbous 'antlers' of the tiny *Cyphonia clavata* (187) is unknown.

186

187

188

189

190

with a wingspan of around five inches.

Often the patterning on the underside of a butterfly's wings is similar to that of the upper side, but in more subdued colors, or at least in colors that will afford better protection. The purple emperor, *Apatura iris*, replaces the vivid purple of the upper side with an apparently equally striking pattern of white, brown and orange; but this pattern is remarkably hard to detect in the woodlands in which it lives. On the other hand, butterflies that already have somber colorings on the upper surfaces of their wings generally have very similar colors on the lower surface. An example is the woodland grayling, *Hipparchia fagi*, patterned somberly above and below in shades of brown, pale yellow and white. Indeed, some of the graylings, such as Freyer's grayling, *Hipparchia fatua*, show in the males more vivid coloring on the underside than the upper. The upper wing surface in this species is a very dark brown, faintly shaded. The very evenness of the color might make it easy to spot among the woodlands of the Balkans

and the Levant, where it lives. The underside, more strikingly patterned and showing white streaks and two yellow eyes, provides disruptive coloration which makes detection difficult.

By contrast with butterflies, most moths rest with their wings either spread out, or with the upper wings folded over the lower ones. Their protective coloration is therefore necessary on the upper wing surfaces, and often on the front wings only. The undersurface and the hind wings may be much more vividly colored, and are frequently lighter in color than the upper surface. For example, the ilia underwing, *Catocala ilia*, rests with its bright red and purple hind wings concealed by the upper wings, which are gray and mottled like the bark of the trees on which it settles.

The shape of an insect also helps it to hide from predators. The most familiar examples are the stick and leaf insects of the order Phasmida. Walking sticks, indeed, not only have bodies shaped like twigs, but they take up attitudes that resemble

189. 190. The immobile pupal stage of the Lepidoptera is potentially the most hazardous part of their life history. In many species, including the Trinidadian orange dog butterfly (*Papilio anchisiades*) shown in these two pictures, the pupa (chrysalis) is placed in a prominent place but so well disguised as to deceive the keenest eye. Both from the side (189) and the top (190) the resemblance to a broken, lichen-covered twig is perfect.

191

192

193

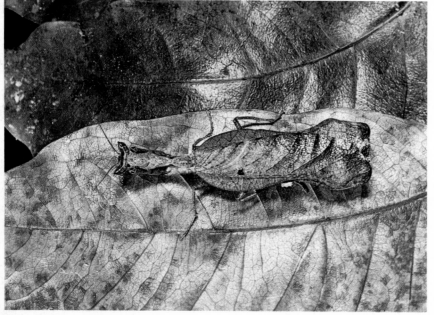

the position in which you would expect to find a twig. Katydids and grasshoppers similarly have long, thin bodies which enable them to blend into the landscape of grass stems and long, spear-like leaves among which they make their homes. The caterpillars of many geometrid moths also resemble twigs, and like the stick insects they remain motionless to complete the illusion. It is not only the caterpillars that are capable of remaining inert in this way. The adult Chinese character moth, *Cilix glaucata*, passes the daylight hours on a leaf with its wings folded and looking exactly like a bird dropping. As night falls the 'bird dropping' spreads its wings and takes to the air. *Cilix* is one of several moths that have adopted this form of camouflage. The caterpillars of some swallowtail butterflies also resemble bird droppings; during the day, when they do not feed, they rest fully exposed and motionless on the upper surface of the leaves of the food plant.

The ability to freeze in this way is often used by insects to avoid detection, since nothing catches the eye so quickly as movement. Many beetles when disturbed allow themselves to fall to the ground, where they draw in their legs and antennae and remain perfectly still, looking remarkably like small stones or particles of soil. The pupal stage, in which so many immature insects are at their most vulnerable, is rendered safer by the fact that a pupating insect rarely moves, and therefore does nothing to attract unwelcome attentions. Weevils in the genus *Cionus* feed on the leaves of figwort, a plant which forms parchment-colored, spherical seedcases. During pupation, the *Cionus* larvae make cocoons exactly resembling the seedcases, and locate them among the real ones – an example of 'see no weevil'!

Other methods of protection
The ground, with its litter of twigs, fallen leaves, and other debris in the woodlands, and the tangle of grasses and other close-growing plants in the open, is one of the safest places for concealment, and many insects make their homes there. Indeed, the normal dwelling places of many insects provide a very large measure of safety. Such places include under the bark of fallen logs, beneath stones, or in the crevices of tree-trunks.

To get some idea of how well hidden the world of insects is, try making an active search for them. Crevices in damp places, basements, or even the corners of a bathroom probably conceal silverfish, and if you are unlucky, your wardrobe may conceal tiny clothes moths, with their larvae eating your winter suits. Any board or stone slab lying in the garden will certainly have insects beneath it, especially earwigs, springtails and beetles.

A heap of wet, rotting leaf-mold provides home for the maggots of flies, and a manure or compost heap will conceal many other grubs or eggs, depending on the time of year. Caterpillars, aphids and other insects can be found in summer on the undersides of leaves. A fallen log is a very rich hunting ground, both in summer and in winter. Cold weather shelterers beneath the bark include such insects as queen wasps and the grubs of craneflies and beetles. In summer you may find adult beetles, ants, and the maggots of those flies

194

191–4. For a naturalist there can be few experiences more thrilling than the first visit to the tropics. Although the members of OSF have traveled widely, the first filming trip to Trinidad in the winter of 1974 was an unforgettable experience. The great number of species, the abundance of individuals, their beauty and the perfection of their adaptations all made a profound impression. The insects shown here passed unnoticed in their natural habitat and were only seen when attracted to the mercury vapor lights of the moth trap.

The notodontid moth *Astylis besckei* (191), the mantid *Acanthops falcata* (193) and another unnamed moth (194) all hide by day among fallen leaves. The moth *Rhuda* sp. (192) lies inconspicuously on lichen covered twigs.

which produce several generations in one season. The ground beneath the log will almost certainly reveal more insects in various stages of development. Rocks submerged in ponds and brooks are also favorite places of concealment, hiding the naiads of stoneflies and the larvae of some midges.

Closely allied to protective coloring is the idea of bluff – making an enemy decide that its prey is bigger, tougher, or otherwise less desirable than it in fact is. The outstanding example of bluff is shown by the caterpillar of the puss moth, *Cerura vinula*. This caterpillar is large and succulent in appearance, colored a bright green that matches the vegetation on which it feeds, and with a purple patch on its back which serves as disruptive camouflage. If despite this disguise the caterpillar is disturbed or threatened, it raises its head to reveal a brilliant red and orange face with two dark spots that resemble eyes, enough to put any bird off its food. At the same time the caterpillar raises its harmless tail appendages and waves them around as if they were stings.

Some adult moths also have conspicuous eyespots on their wings, which give the impression that the insect is just part of a much larger and fiercer looking creature. Eyespots are also common among butterflies, but because a butterfly sits with its wings folded upwards, it generally has a pair of eyespots on each wing so that they appear as a pair of eyes from either side.

Bluff of this kind often helps to ward off predators but if all else fails, then there is one recourse left: to escape from danger. The legs and wings that carry an insect to its food can also serve to carry it away from a predator. If you have ever tried to swat a fly or catch a butterfly in a net – or better still, watched a bird trying to catch a moth – you will know exactly how effective wings can be. For this reason, birds that prey on flying insects, such as the swallow, swift, and martin, are very fast fliers indeed, so that they can overhaul their quarry and snap it up before it can take evasive action.

There are many swift runners among the insects,

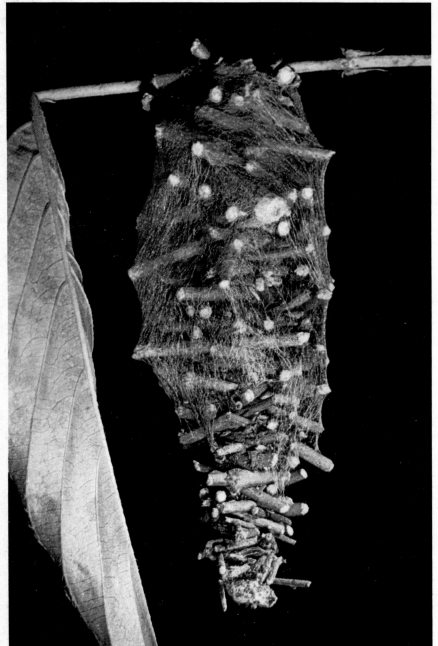

195

196

197

195, 196. Another form of concealment is to build some form of 'house' or other inert covering. The bagworm moths (Psychidae) (195) construct a portable case of leaf and twig fragments in which the caterpillar lives.

The green lacewings (Chrysopidae) belong to the order Neuroptera. The larvae feed mainly on aphids and cover themselves with the husks of past meals (196) for concealment.

197. Concealment as a means of protection is mainly of benefit to those insects that are not distasteful and that lack other means of defense. Wasps like these *Polystes* possess a powerful sting and advertise the fact by their conspicuous livery of black and yellow stripes.

notably cockroaches, silverfish, ants, and ground beetles. Leaping to safety is another way of escaping an enemy, and if you have had the misfortune to have to try to catch a flea you will remember the episode as the original now-you-see-it, now-you-don't event. Fleas, flea-beetles, crickets and grasshoppers have specially developed back legs which enable them to spring incredible distances in relation to their size. A grasshopper, for example, can jump a distance twenty times its own body length, and can do a high jump of half that distance – that is, the equivalent of a moderately tall man jumping a height of sixty feet. Investigations with a slow-motion camera suggest that a grasshopper's thigh muscle is indeed more powerful than any other muscle in the animal kingdom. Several other insects leap by entirely different mechanisms. The springtails of the order Collembola rely on a forked springing organ which is folded forward under the abdomen and held by a kind of catch. When the springtail is alarmed the catch flies open and the

springing organ strikes the ground, propelling the insect through the air. The larva of the cheesefly, *Piopila casei*, grasps the tail end of its body in its mouthparts and tensions its body like a spring. When it lets go, the released tension hurtles the insect into space.

Click beetles, also sometimes called skipjacks (Elateridae), have their own springing mechanism which is not found in any other group of insects. Like many other members of the beetle order, a click beetle will if disturbed drop to the ground as though it has been shot, landing as a rule on its back. After lying still for a few moments the beetle will suddenly stretch, there is a sharp clicking sound, and the insect leaps several inches into the air, landing as a rule the right way up so that it can scuttle to safety.

The springing mechanism consists of a projecting spine on the underside of the prothorax – the front thoracic segment – which engages in a cavity on the underside of the next segment, the mesothorax. When the beetle arches its back the spring is released, causing its wing-cases to strike the ground and hurl the beetle into the air.

Burrowing into the ground is another method used to evade unwelcome attentions. As we have seen, a great many insects dig down to make safe nesting places for their eggs, and for the larvae to develop when they hatch. Ants, termites and many species of bees, wasps and beetles all make their homes underground. There they are safe from all except burrowing or digging predators; however, anteaters make short work of the nests of ants and termites, and even a wasp's nest hidden in a bank may be torn apart by the iron-hard claws of a badger, whose dense fur makes it impervious to stings.

Mimicry

We have seen how some insects such as the stick insects are so made and colored that they exactly resemble their backgrounds. This is just one aspect of a much larger subject in the realms of defense and concealment – mimicry, a close resemblance not between an insect and its environment, but between one insect and another.

Generally the mimicry is that of appearance, though in the hidden world of insects mimicry of sound and scent is also found. There is some mimicry in other classes of the animal kingdom, notably among snakes; but insects are by far the best mimics. Usually, the mimic has copied an insect that is poisonous or not a desirable food for some other reason. The mimic itself may or may not be palatable to a bird or other predator.

There are two basic kinds of mimicry, and they are called Batesian mimicry and Müllerian mimicry after the two distinguished zoologists who first noted and described them. Batesian mimicry was observed by the English naturalist Henry Walter Bates (1825–92) in the course of a visit to the Amazon River region of Brazil. In this form of mimicry, the mimic gains an advantage by appearing to be a distasteful or harmful insect. Müllerian mimicry was also noted in Brazil, by the German zoologist Fritz Müller (1821–97), one of the earliest supporters of Charles Darwin's theories of evolution. Müllerian mimicry is the similarity that two or more harmful species have to one another.

The advantage of Batesian mimicry is obvious; but what is the benefit of Müllerian mimicry? It is much greater than you might imagine, and has been likened to the effect of a business cartel or monopoly. Obviously, for predators such as birds to learn that a certain species of insect is bad to eat, the predators first have to sample one and find out the hard way . . . a hard way for the victims, too. If a young bird has to try an insect of each inedible species before it can learn to reject them all, there is bound to be a considerable mortality among the inedible insects. However, if they all wear the same uniform, the bird will recognize it after only one or two attempts to eat the insects, and therefore the death-rate among the prey will be greatly reduced. The risk and the loss have both been shared.

As you can see, there is a positive advantage at all times for insects adopting Müllerian mimicry: they cut their losses by its means. Both the model – the species copied – and the mimics benefit. But

198

199

the models in Batesian mimicry do not gain any advantage at all: in fact, the reverse is the case. If a bird, for example, finds that most insects with certain coloring are good to eat, it is likely to continue to prey on such insects, and not be put off by the occasional unpleasant mouthful. In this kind of mimicry it is therefore important that the mimic should be much less numerous than its model. Some species of predators acquire an apparent taste for insects that other birds reject. The cuckoo, a bird with admittedly eccentric habits anyway, feeds on hairy caterpillars, which other birds normally shun. It also eats the larvae of the magpie moth, *Abraxas grossulariata*, brightly-colored caterpillars which infest currant and gooseberry bushes. These caterpillars are notoriously unpopular, and experiments with a wide range of insect-eating animals, including other birds, bats, frogs and lizards, have proved that the caterpillars are rejected every time, except by cuckoos.

Warning colors are generally displayed by

198, 199. The social wasps all gain mutual protection by having similar markings, which predators very quickly learn to avoid. However a number of non-venomous insects have also adopted similar markings, thereby acquiring protection by mimicry. The European wasp beetle *Clytus arietis* (198) enhances its appearance by its extremely wasp-like movements.

The currant moth *Abraxas grossulariata* has an unpleasant bitter taste and is avoided by birds. The pupa (199) is also distasteful, advertising the fact by its wasp-like markings.

200

201

202

insects that are active during the day. Most nocturnal moths, for example, are dull in color, with no particular indications of taste. It is not surprising, therefore, to find mimicry common among butterflies and those moths that fly by day. Generally speaking, mimicry is found more often among females than among males; this is probably because the female is more vulnerable than the male when she is laying eggs and therefore unable to escape danger by taking wing. In many species, both sexes are mimics, but in such cases the female's mimicry is often more complete – in other words, she is more heavily disguised.

The butterflies that are mimicked belong to a few subfamilies, which contain many unpalatable species. Chief among these is the subfamily Danainae, which belongs to the family Nymphalidae, the brush-footed butterflies. Some zoologists make a separate family of this group, the Danaidae. These generally large butterflies have an unpleasant smell as well as an unpleasant taste, and their bodies are tough and leathery.

Among this group is the monarch butterfly, *Danaus plexippus*, whose amazing migratory habits are described on page 63. In North America there lives another butterfly known as the viceroy, *Limenitis archippus*, a close relative of the white admiral, *Limenitis camilla*, of Europe. The male viceroy, like the white admiral, is a sober-looking insect which has blackish-brown upper sides to its wings, marked with white. But the females appear in the full regalia of a monarch, orange and yellow, marked with brown and white.

Regional influences

Nearly-related species often mimic different models, and this apparently is because they copy only models that are plentiful in the areas where they live. *Papilio dardanus* is a species of swallowtail butterfly living in Africa. Its females have been found mimicking at least six models with very different wing-patterning. As you can imagine, all this complex camouflage causes great problems for entomologists trying to sort out the different species.

Mimicry among butterflies is most widespread in the tropics, and it is there, too, that butterflies are most often eaten by birds. The majority of the most vividly colored butterflies occur in tropical forests, where the great contrasts of light and shade, and the strong golden light of the sun, tend to make vivid colors hard to spot. But there is plenty of mimicry in temperate regions, too, and among a great variety of insects.

One of the best-known examples of mimicry is provided by the hoverflies (Syrphidae). Hoverflies are true flies, and completely harmless as far as predators are concerned. But many of them are banded black and yellow like wasps, and some have even developed an apparent wasp waist so that shape helps coloration in deceiving the enemy. Some species are distinctly hairy and resemble bees. *Volucella bombylans* even occurs in several distinct color forms so that more than one kind of bee is imitated.

Flies are not the only insects that imitate wasps and bees. Some beetles and moths do so, too. For example, the bee hawk moths, genus *Hemaris*,

200. *Dasymutilla klugi* is a velvet ant from the Arizona desert. The red and black markings of this wingless female advertize her exceedingly painful sting.

201. The broad-bordered bee hawk moth (*Hemaris fuciformis*) is one of the few day flying members of the family Sphingidae. The scales on the wings are shed soon after emergence. In flight these moths are quite like bumblebees.

202, 203. One of the best examples of mimicry encountered by OSF was in south-western Arizona. The wasp *Polystes comanchus* (202) emerges when the sunflowers bloom after the summer rains. This wasp is mimicked by the neuropteran *Climaciella brunnea* (203) which belongs to the family Mantispidae. Mantispids, which are usually brown or green in color, have raptorial front legs like those of praying mantises and are parasitic as larvae on other insects and spiders.

204. The seven-spot ladybird *Coccinella septempunctata* is brightly marked to advertize its distastefulness. Its smooth, rounded shape makes it safe from attack by predators such as spiders.

205. The Trinidadian assassin bug *Rasahus hamatus* has a painful bite and like many of its relatives is distinctively marked.

203

204   205

206, 207. *Syssphinx molina* is a saturniid moth from Trinidad, which in the normal resting position (207) looks quite like a hawk moth (Sphingidae). When disturbed *S. molina* thrusts the front wings forward to reveal a pair of large, brightly marked eye spots. This flash display of eye spots is sufficient to frighten off many predators.

206

207

have stout furry bodies and in flight as well as on the ground could be taken at first glance for bees. The locust borer, which is a beetle, resembles a wasp. Another group of beetles, the family Lycidae, are known as net-winged beetles, because they have a superficial resemblance to the nerve-winged insects of the order Neuroptera. The Neuroptera are well-known as predators, so this may be an example of protective mimicry, for the net-winged beetles have soft bodies and are very slow-moving, which would render them liable to destruction by predators. As an additional precaution the net-winged beetles are colored red, orange, or yellow, sometimes with black markings. A further stage in mimicry is provided by at least one species of moth, which closely resembles one Peruvian kind of net-winged beetle!

Ants are also the subject of mimicry, particularly by beetles. The family Anthicidae have the popular name of ant-like flower beetles for just this reason. Some bugs also imitate ants. Just to

208. *Automeris memusae* is another South American saturniid moth with eye spots on the hind wings.

209. The cinnabar moth (*Hypocrita jacobaeae*) is inedible to birds, probably because the larvae feed on ragwort. It has bright markings and flies slowly so predators recognize it.

210, 211. *Dirphia avia* is another South American saturniid moth which at rest is drab and inconspicuous (210). When a predator attacks, the moth thrusts its wings forward and arches its body to display brilliant black and orange hairs arranged in bands across the abdomen (211).

210

add to the entomologist's headaches, several genera of spiders also mimic ants, going so far as to hold up their front legs as if they were antennae so that they appear to possess only the correct insect complement of six legs.

Evolution of mimicry

How has all this mimicry come about? It is not, of course, a deliberate or conscious act on the part of the insects. It is an example of natural selection in progress, the process expounded by Charles Darwin in his revolutionary *Origin of Species* back in the 1850s. Just as various orders and species of insects have evolved over millions of years to fill certain niches in the systems of plants and animals in which they live, adapting to eat the food available and live in the prevailing conditions, so some species have adapted for survival in a world of hunters and hunted.

The process by which this happens is called *mutation*. A mutation is an accidental variation in the genes which form part of the nucleus of the cells of the body. Once a mutation has taken place, it is faithfully copied in all succeeding generations, and a varied form of the original is evolved. A mutation occurs relatively infrequently, but over many millions of years and millions of generations, changes take place and become stabilized.

The reason for a changed form becoming established is because that form is better suited to the conditions of life for the particular species. We do not know what hoverflies looked like millions of years ago, but it is likely that they were very different from those of today. They survived because there were fewer birds to prey on them. But gradually mutation produced hoverflies that looked more and more like wasps. The process of natural selection meant that those hoverflies which looked least like wasps were eaten more than those which resembled their less edible cousins. This process is sometimes called survival of the fittest, but the word fittest needs to be read with caution.

211

Evolution by natural selection takes a very long time, and though we can see its results we cannot always follow the chain of events. Fortunately there is one excellent example that has taken place within the past hundred years: the transformation of the peppered moth, *Biston betularia*. This moth is normally a pale mottled gray in color – just the right shade to go against the lichen-covered bark of a tree and pass unnoticed.

Many years ago entomologists noticed that there were two varieties of the peppered moth, the second variety having dark, sooty colored wings. Investigations showed that apart from the color there was no difference in the moths: they were merely varieties of the same species. What was important was the fact that the dark moths occurred in towns, and the light-colored ones in the country. In towns, particularly industrial ones, nearly everything is polluted with soot, which turns the ground, the trunks of trees, and even leaves a dark color. In such a setting the ordinary moth shows up clearly when it takes up its normal resting posture against a tree trunk. The dark-colored varieties, on the other hand, blend into the background.

Research has shown that between the two kinds of peppered moths there is just one different gene – the one that controls the deposition of the black pigment, melanin. Melanic moths are the result of a mutation and occur in quite a few species. Melanic specimens of the peppered moth first appeared in the 1850s. In the towns the dark moths survived while their lighter brethren were eaten; in clean surroundings the lighter moths survived while the dark ones perished. Examples of dark and light moths in each others' territories may result from a number of causes, including migration.

A final proof that this change was an evolutionary one has been provided in recent years in areas where there has been a marked decrease in pollution; in these cleaned-up areas the proportion of light-colored peppered moths is beginning to increase; melanic moths are on the wane.

Chapter 6

The Social Insects

Basically, insects are solitary animals. They live by themselves for themselves, meeting only to mate. Often, the offspring are abandoned by the mother, who may be dead before her eggs have hatched. Yet there are exceptions to this rule of solitude, as anyone will know who has walked through a cloud of midges on a summer evening.

Even so, a cloud of midges is a cloud of individuals. Gregariousness, the herd instinct, draws many species of insects together. There are several reasons for such behavior. The midges swarm in a mating flight for a brief period of their lives, and then the swarm gradually disperses as couples pair off and leave to mate. Mayflies swarm in a similar manner.

Other insects are found in large numbers close to their food supply. Aphids are found in their thousands on garden plants: so are caterpillars of such species as the cabbage white butterfly. The larvae of insects which lay large numbers of eggs all hatch at about the same time, and so groups occur at this stage of their lives. Migration brings huge numbers of insects together, such as swarms of locusts, or flocks of butterflies.

None of these aggregations of insects is in any sense of the word a society. There is no organization about their assembly, merely coincidence or perhaps a sharing of interests. However, the hidden world of insects contains four kinds of insects which have very highly organized societies – so complex in their structure that only man and a few other mammals have anything to compare. Three of these insects belong to the order Hymenoptera – bees, wasps, and ants; the other social insects are the termites, which form the order Isoptera. All the ants and termites live in societies, but many species of bees and wasps do not, and some have less highly organized communes.

Even zoologists have disagreed about what exactly is meant by the term social insects, but generally it may be said that social insects are those in which the generations overlap, live together, and co-operate in their lives and work. With this goes a caste system, in which individuals of the same species are different in form and function, a difference that is not only one of sex.

Perhaps the easiest way to see how the complex social life evolved is to look at some other members of the Hymenoptera which do not have such a system. This actually includes the majority of species of both wasps and bees. Such bees and wasps are known as solitary bees and wasps, because though they build nests and raise young on the same general principles as the more familiar honey bees, each queen works more or less single-handed, as it were, to raise her brood.

Solitary wasps and bees

Some solitary bees and wasps are parasites, and do not build nests. The rest all construct nests or cells, on varying patterns and of assorted materials. A typical solitary wasp is an egg-laying queen, which builds her nest and stocks its cells with paralyzed insects. The wasp paralyzes her victims with her sting, the poison from which has preservative qualities. Many of the victims remain alive but helpless. The bodies of those which succumb remain fresh long enough for the wasp's purpose, which is to feed the larvae when they hatch. Most wasps are particular about which kind of insect they put in the pantry. For example, the potter wasps of the genus *Eumenes* select small caterpillars; the spider-hunters, *Pompilus*, and tarantula hawks, *Pepsis*, capture spiders; and other species choose flies, weevils and bees.

The nests of solitary wasps vary greatly in design and structure. Each small nest is provisioned with a paralyzed caterpillar. The wasp lays an egg in it, sealing it up with mud to keep out predators. Mud is also used by members of the subfamily Eumeninae this time to form cells inside tunnels which they bore into wood or make in hollow stalks. Wasps of the genus *Odynerus* dig tunnels in the ground and make cells within them, each provisioned with an insect to supply food for the egg that is laid in it.

A step towards a more social life is taken by some species in the Eumeninae: instead of sealing up the cells when they are provisioned, the wasp leaves them open, and takes fresh supplies to the larvae as they grow and develop. But there is no further contact between mother and offspring, and so there is no true social life as such.

Some solitary bees lead lives similar to those of the solitary wasps. Unlike the social bees, solitary bees do not make wax, but construct their nests of vegetable material of various kinds, using holes in the ground, tree and plant cavities, and any other suitable sites; the choice varies according to

212–27. *Apis mellifera*, the honey bee, is usually photographed through the glass of observation hives. To avoid picture degradation arising from reflection and dirt, OSF designed and made a special hive in which the glass cover could be removed for direct photography on to the comb. A docile strain of bee was used but even so great care was necessary to avoid vibration. Bees also dislike drafts, so the cameraman, whose face was inches from the comb, had literally to hold his breath! The queen (212) is the one indispensable member of every honey-bee colony. Without a mated queen a colony dwindles away as its members die of old age and are not replaced. The queen also provides a cohesive force by secreting a substance which keeps the thousands of workers contented. Always the center of attention, the queen is groomed and fed by the workers in her vicinity.

213

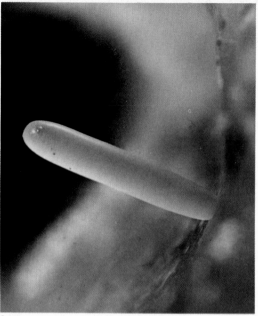

214

215

The sole function of the drone, that is the male (213), is to fertilize young queens during mating flights. Males are produced in limited numbers during summer; towards autumn they are denied access to stored honey and are dragged outside the hive to die of starvation. When laying her eggs the queen wanders over the comb investigating cells; she lays an egg (214) attached to the base of each empty cell she encounters.

species. The cells are also made from vegetable material, several to a nest, and provisioned with pollen soaked in honey, a substance known as bee-bread. The nest is then sealed off, and like so many other insects the bee is generally dead before her offspring mature.

The commonest members of this group of bees are the leaf-cutters, which are in the genus *Megachile*. They cut oval pieces of leaf and roll them around masses of pollen to form cells shaped like small thimbles. Once she has laid her egg, the bee then seals the thimble with another piece of leaf, this time cut in a perfect circle. The mason bee, another relative, constructs rugged nests made of what is virtually concrete – soil mixed with a salivary secretion, strengthened with small embedded pebbles. Usually, the rock-hard nest is the size and shape of half an orange.

Bumblebees

There are many variations on the social theme, and one of the simpler organizations is that of the

bumblebees, belonging to the genus *Bombus*. Queen bumblebees hibernate during the winter, emerging in spring to look for a suitable nesting site. This is generally a ready-made hole, perhaps one formerly used by some burrowing animal such as a meadow mouse. The bumblebee lines her nest with moss, dry grasses and leaves; most species have this nest deep in a tunnel, but some, the so-called carder bees, braid together grass and similar material and make a surface nest carefully hidden in the surrounding vegetation. Once the nest is made the bumblebee secretes wax, from which she makes a cup-shaped egg cell. Inside the cell the bee places a ball of pollen, and then lays about a dozen eggs on it, covering the whole cell with a wax dome. Near the entrance to the nest the bumblebee queen constructs a wax honey-pot, almost as big as a thimble, which she fills with honey. The eggs hatch after a few days, producing small white grubs. These grubs feed on the pollen ball, and as they use it up the queen provides more. She also enlarges the cell to provide room for the growing grubs. In due course the grubs pupate, and about twenty days after the eggs were laid adult bees emerge from the pupal cases.

Here we have the first example of different types of adults, the beginnings of the caste system on which the organization of the social insects' world is based. The new adults are females, but smaller than the queen: they are worker-bees. The queen goes on to make more cells and lay more eggs; the workers gradually take over the duties of feeding the newly-hatched larvae, and foraging for nectar and pollen. As the numbers of workers increase, the queen does little but lay eggs.

For most of her life the queen lays fertilized eggs – fertilized from the sperm reserve she acquired when she mated at the end of the previous season. As the summer goes on, the queen lays a mixture of fertilized and unfertilized eggs. The unfertilized eggs produce male bees; the larvae of the fertilized eggs are given extra rations, and produce not workers but young queens. Some workers lay unfertilized eggs, which produce males.

In the temperate parts of the world bumblebee

colonies last only for the summer season, a period of six or seven months. With the onset of autumn the young queens mate, and look for somewhere to hibernate. The rest of the colony, which may number 100 workers or more, lingers on until the coming of the cold weather kills off the bees, leaving only the queens to winter-over and carry on the line.

Apart from size and better development of the ovaries, there is not a great deal of difference between the worker bumblebees and their queen. There are size differences among the workers, however, and generally the larger bees go foraging, while the smaller ones tend the eggs and larvae. For comfort the nest needs to be kept at a reasonable temperature, and the great danger is not cold but overheating. To prevent the temperature rising above, say, 80°, workers stand near the entrance, fanning cool air into the nest.

Stingless bees
Bumblebee colonies are small, about 400 bees normally being the upper limit – though at least one nest of more than 2,000 bees has been recorded. Much larger colonies are formed by stingless bees, of the genera *Melipona* and *Tripona*. These bees are comparatively small, and though they do in fact have stings these organs are too small to be effective against man. *Melipona* produce colonies up to 4,000 strong, while *Tripona* colonies may have up to 80,000 bees. The stingless bees live in the tropics and some subtropical regions. Their mode of life is much more like that of the honey bees.

A typical nest is constructed in a hollow tree, though other cavities are used including deserted termite nests. There is a battery of brood cells, where the eggs are laid and hatched, and a series of storage pots for honey and pollen. A wall of mud or other material – called batumen, from a Brazilian word for wall – closes off the cavity, or, if the nest is exposed, surrounds it entirely.

Stingless bee nests are perennial, and the warm climate in which these bees flourish allows for activity all the year round. When the nest becomes overcrowded worker scouts begin searching for a new nesting site, and once they have found it they begin construction. Material for the new nest is ferried from the old one, and walls, brood cells, and honey pots are built. Meanwhile back at the nest another group of workers has been rearing a young queen. When the new nest is all ready for occupation, the young queen flies to it. Male bees from the old nest and other nests are waiting around, from which the new queen soon chooses a mate, makes her mating flight, and settles down to lay her first eggs.

Honey bees
A flourishing honey-bee hive contains between 50,000 and 80,000 bees. In it live one queen, several hundred males, known as drones, and the workers, which form the balance. The three castes of bees are more strongly differentiated in the honey bees than in the stingless bees. The drone is a solid, chunky-looking insect with very large eyes. The queen is longer, but not so thickset. The worker is a compact-looking insect, much smaller

216

217

than the queen. The queen's only duty is to lay eggs, and she performs no other task in the hive. The drones exist only to fertilize new queens at the appropriate time; they do no work, and exist on stores of honey provided by the workers, which carry out all the rest of the hive's activities.

The queen makes her mating flight very early in her life. Three or four days later she is ready to begin laying eggs, and she spends the rest of her life in this task. The workers prepare brood cells, and the queen wanders about the comb or combs within the brood area, a region of the nest where the temperature is not lower than about 85°. She lays an egg in each cell she finds empty. The queen honey bee has no abilities other than egg-laying; she cannot build cells, or even forage for food. The workers feed her from time to time on broodfood, a highly nutritious substance secreted from special glands. This food is not the same as that which the workers supply to each other, which is regurgitated nectar or honey.

One of the mysteries of a queen bee's life is how

The eggs hatch in three to four days and the larvae destined to be workers (216) are fed for the first three days on a protein-rich food secreted by worker bees. On the fourth day pollen and nectar are added to the diet and growth is complete on or about the fifth day. The workers now cap the cells with wax (217).

Shortly afterwards the larva changes to a pupa which at first is white (218 – wax cap removed), but which gradually darkens. On about the thirteenth day after pupation the young adult sheds the pupal skin (219). As soon as the mandibles are hardened the new recruit chews through the wax cap and emerges on to the comb (220) where she is groomed and fed by other workers (221).

218

219

221

220

she regulates her egg-laying so that in each cell designed for a worker she lays a fertilized egg, and in each slightly larger cell built for a drone she lays an unfertilized one. She rarely makes a mistake – but no one knows what the mechanism is that controls the queen's actions. It may be chemical, or it may be a stimulus derived from the size or shape of the cell itself.

While the queen is in full health and vigor – which may be for anything between three and five years – she will not tolerate a rival, and will put to death any other queen she finds in the nest. When she is failing, however, the story is different.

Although the queen is essential to the life of the hive, because without her there would be no worker bees to carry on its existence, the backbone of the hive is the great body of workers. The workers carry out a great many different duties, and the way in which these are allocated is related partly to the age of each bee, and partly to the immediate needs of the nest. Unlike the queen, the life of a worker bee is measured in weeks or

222

months, rather than years. Workers reared during the summer live for only about six weeks, while those bred in autumn, known as winter bees, may live as many months.

Let us consider first the life of a summer bee, the more usual kind encountered. The first three weeks or so of the bee's life is spent on household duties around the hive. For the first three days she solicits food from older workers, and then supplements this diet with honey and pollen, to which she helps herself from storage cells within the hive. She spends some time cleaning out brood cells ready for re-use, but most of her life at this stage is taken up with resting or moving about the nest, apparently looking to see what work needs to be done. It will be seen that in this way the hive always has a large reserve of labor to call on if there is a crisis.

During these early days the worker also helps to feed the older larvae, until her brood-food glands mature and come into operation, when she transfers her attentions to feeding the younger larvae. By the time she is twelve days old, her wax-

producing glands have come into operation, and the young bee then turns more to building and repairing combs. For the next seven days her duties include storing honey and pollen brought in by the foragers, cleaning the hive, and dragging out the bodies of dead workers. During this period she makes her first flights, mainly practice runs to learn the orientation of the hive and get used to her wings.

At the age of about three weeks the worker gives up her household duties and turns to foraging, spending many hours each day seeking nectar and pollen and bringing them back to the hive. A few bees spend time between flights acting as sentries at the entrance to the hive. After three weeks of this arduous duty most worker bees die.

Although this is the ideal pattern for a bee's life, there are many variations on it, and these seem to depend on the needs of the hive. If there is a shortage of foragers, younger bees are seen hunting for nectar and pollen. If there are too few young bees to run the hive, older workers turn to and tend the

The worker bee carries out an orderly progression of duties in the hive, starting with cleaning out cells (222), then feeding larvae and finally repairing cells and building new comb.

223

By the end of the third week she commences field duties, collecting pollen, which is stored in baskets on the hind legs (215), or nectar (223). The returning forager scrapes off the contents of the pollen baskets into storage cells; the nectar is transmitted by mouth to younger workers (224).

larvae, clean the cells, and feed the queen. At any time, too, there are always a large number of bees resting, and their presence in the hive helps to keep its temperature high so that the larvae can be reared. Bees within the hive actively look for tasks to do, and if they do not find any, they join the foraging force, even though they are much younger than the usual age.

The drones do no work, and are fed by the workers as one of their many duties. Since there are rarely more than a few hundred drones in a hive, this is not such an onerous task as it might seem. Indeed, the workers generally take care to control the number of drones pretty strictly. They have been known to drag surplus drone larvae out of the hive, and to tear down drone cells and rebuild them as worker cells if too many have been constructed.

At all times the workers are conscious of the presence of the queen, and if she dies or is removed from the hive they become restless. A roaring sound may be heard coming from the hive,

224

225

226

227

and this is produced by workers fanning currents of air over their scent-producing glands, possibly in an attempt to keep the hive's identity alive. While the queen is both alive and active this identity is provided by queen substance, a secretion provided by the queen which the workers receive either directly from her, or from another worker which has received it.

When a queen begins to fail, her output of queen substance falls off, and this is the signal to the workers that a new queen is required. At once they begin to build special queen cells, which are larger than those for drones and workers. The eggs laid by the old queen in these cells are apparently identical to those of worker bees. But the larvae when they hatch are fed exclusively on brood-food, and not, like worker bees, for three days on brood-food and then on pollen and nectar. The name royal jelly is sometimes given to this food because of its apparent importance in producing new queens. The amount of food provided for larvae intended to become queens is much greater than that which is provided for workers.

If a hive loses its queen suddenly the workers take emergency action to raise a new one. They convert some worker cells containing young larvae into queen cells, and begin feeding up these larvae to convert them into queens. But to do this there must be a larva available less than three days old. After that it is too late, since the larva is sealed into its cell to pupate at the age of five days. If no young larva is available, the colony generally perishes. But not always. Once the queen substance is no longer available many of the workers take to laying eggs. Because the workers are unfertilized, these eggs produce drones. But once in a while the process of parthenogenesis described in Chapter 3 comes into play, and a worker lays an egg that produces a female. Such a female can be fed to turn into a queen, which can then mate and return to save the colony.

In the hive, the rights of primogeniture are strictly adhered to. The first virgin queen to hatch out seeks out the cells of any other potential

A worker which has found a good source of food conveys information about the direction and distance from the hive by dancing on the comb face. The 'round dance' (225) indicates that food is near at hand. During summer there is much coming and going from the hive (226) and the colony increases in size until swarming occurs. This is the method by which colony reproduction takes place. Workers rear new queens in special cells and before these emerge the old queen departs accompanied by many of the workers. The swarm hangs up (227) while scouts locate a new nesting site.

228

229

230

231

228–43. *Eciton burchelli*, the driver ant. This is a species of New World driver or army ant which exists in colonies of up to a million individuals, of which most are workers. These are supported by several thousand soldiers and the whole colony is dependent on a single queen.

The army ants are voracious carnivores which lead a nomadic existence in the forest, hunting during the day and forming a nest, or bivouac, composed of strands of ants with legs interlinked, at night (228). At intervals of two to three weeks the ants enter a resident phase in which they remain in one camp for two weeks or so. Each morning foraging parties of ants stream out into the surrounding forest, following

queens and breaks them open. The workers then destroy her rivals for her. If two queens hatch at the same time they fight to the death, the survivor taking over the leadership of the colony. However, a young queen, newly mated, and an old and failing queen may co-exist for several weeks in perfect harmony, sharing the task of egg-laying until the old queen eventually dies.

Sometimes the presence of a new queen is the prelude to the foundation of a new colony, a process known as swarming. Nobody knows all the reasons that trigger off swarming, but they appear to include overcrowding. Before a swarm takes place life in the colony changes. Queen cells are built – though not invariably – and the old queen reduces her egg production. Then, possibly a few days before the new queens are due to hatch, about half the bees in the hive rise into the air in a body, taking the old queen and some of the drones with them. This vast body of bees, which may be as many as 30,000 strong, clusters on some convenient perch such as a tree while scouts seek out

a new home. When enough scouts report back to the main swarm that a suitable nesting place has been found, the whole body flies off to take up residence. Many of the workers carry supplies of nectar with them so that they can survive for a few days without foraging.

Occasionally there is a secondary, smaller swarm, known as an afterswarm, which cannot be attributed to overcrowding. This is generally made by bees accompanying a young queen which is escaping before the fight to the death routine.

Communication

As we have seen, a great deal of communication among bees is by way of smell, and the presence of the pheromones described in Chapter 3. But there is a further language of bees which was discovered by the great German zoologist Karl von Frisch – the language by which they communicate the location of pollen and nectar to each other. A bee returning with food from a newly discovered source performs a dance when it reaches the hive. There

232

are two types of dance. One, called a 'round dance' by von Frisch, consists of running rapidly on the surface of a comb and tracing out a series of figure-eights. This dance is performed when the source of food is fairly close to the hive, up to 160 feet distant. If the source of food is much further away the bee performs a different routine, which von Frisch called the 'tail-wagging dance.' The bee runs a short distance forward in a straight line, wagging its abdomen rapidly from side to side. It then makes a complete circle to the left and repeats the tail-wagging routine, following this by a complete circle to the right. It then performs the whole routine over and over again.

After a long series of observations and experiments von Frisch and his helpers cracked the bees' code. If the bee performs the straight, wagging run upwards on the surface of the comb, it means 'Fly towards the sun to reach the food.' If the run is downwards, it means 'Fly away from the sun to reach the food.' And if the bee directs its run by several degrees to the left or right of the vertical,

then the direction of the food is that much to right or left of the path to or from the sun. When the other worker bees emerge from the darkness of the hive, they pick up their bearings by the sun and fly straight to the source of food. In experiments von Frisch found that once one bee had located a dish of sugar-water set out as a lure, within minutes dozens, perhaps hundreds, of other bees would be along to collect food.

How does the bee recognize the direction of the sun, especially in cloudy weather? Further experiments have shown that the bee's eyes can detect the plane of polarization of light. In the dark of the hive, gravity can be detected, and the dance is always performed on a vertical surface. If the comb is turned on its side, the bees become disorientated.

Ants
Wonderful though the organization of the bees' social structure may appear, it takes second place to that of the ants. The ants have a more complex

scent trails laid down by the leaders and reinforced by those that follow. Ultimately the ants fan out over the forest floor (229) where they overcome, by stinging, any animal, large or small, which cannot escape. Cockroaches, spiders, bushcrickets and the nests of other kinds of ants seem to be the commonest prey in Trinidad where these pictures were taken. It was noticeable that stick insects were not molested, because they emit a repugnant odor and also they remain motionless. The presence of army ants on the hunt for food is revealed by a general exodus of all animals as they flee for their lives. Towards evening the ants stream back to their nest bearing their spoils (230, 231, 232).

233

234

Large prey is torn apart and carried piecemeal. The largest portions are carried by the smaller soldiers, which can be distinguished by their paler heads and larger jaws. The largest soldiers have extremely long jaws and their duty is to guard the column (238–9). Drivers are very sensitive to vibration and an incautious step or snapping twig will cause the column to break up as the ants fan out to find the source of the disturbance. Woe betide the cameraman who tarries too long; the sting and bite are very painful and a few ants will put a human to flight. Driver ants will also raid wasps' nests (233) and despite possessing stings the wasps never resist but hang up in clusters on adjacent vegetation while the drivers make off with the entire nest contents of eggs, grubs and pupae.

When moving camp the drivers carry their larvae and pupae, which are enclosed in cocoons, to the new home (234–7). Gaps on the trail are bridged by ants which link their claws together so that others can walk across their bodies. In this instance the drivers dispossessed wasps to gain not only food but a sheltered home and we watched for 6½ hours as the drivers filed into the tree. The queen undergoes a cycle of reproduction every few weeks and this coincides with the resident phase when a permanent camp is set up.

235

caste system, and various kinds have armies, cultivate gardens, and even keep aphids, as 'cows.'

As with the bees, ants have three basic castes: queen, worker – who is female – and male. Queens and males have wings, workers do not. Young queens and males mate on the wing; after the mating flight the male, like the male bee, dies. The queen then sets about establishing a nest, or taking over one already in existence. As soon as the mating flight is over the queen removes her wings, rubbing them against twigs or stones and pulling at them with her jaws until they fall off. Once this is done the queen hurries to find a nesting site, generally below ground. There she establishes herself in seclusion, living on reserves of food within her body, including the now useless wing muscles, and lays her eggs.

When the eggs hatch the queen feeds the larvae on saliva for a few days until they pupate. The ants that hatch are a small kind of worker called a minim. The minims at once get to work, breaking out of the nest and foraging for food. The

queen can then devote the rest of her life to egg-laying, drawing on the reserves of sperm from the one mating, which can last her a lifetime of ten years or more. The workers now take over all the duties of tending the larvae and running the nest.

The queen usually becomes very much larger than the workers. In some species she is so large that she could not tend even the first batch of eggs. In the genus *Carebara* the workers are so small they can hitch a ride when the queen goes on her mating flight, clinging to hairs on her legs. When the queen establishes her nest, which she does inside a termite nest, the little workers she has brought with her take on the task of caring for the eggs and larvae right away, and possibly forage for food too.

The workers are not necessarily all alike. In many species they vary greatly in size, and are referred to as majors and minors. The duties carried out by the worker ants vary as do those of the worker bees, but there does not appear to be such a strong relationship of age to duties. The largest

236

237

ants, in species where there is more than one size, have very large, strong mandibles, and are referred to as soldiers. They actually guard the nest, and one or more may generally be seen on duty at the entrance. Workers coming in with food have to touch feelers before they are allowed in.

One of the biggest differences between worker ants and worker bees is that the ants have a very much longer life span. Many species live for five or six years, and a few for much more. Others have lives measured in months and weeks. There is a very wide variation in the population size of an ant colony. Some of the simplest species, such as those in the family Ponerinae living in New Guinea, may have fifty or fewer members in each colony, while army ants of the Central American species *Eciton burchelli* have populations of up to 700,000.

A typical ant's nest has several chambers inside. In one the queen spends her time laying eggs, and being fed and groomed by workers. The eggs are taken off to another chamber, or chambers, for hatching, and the larvae are moved to fresh quarters which form a nursery. Other chambers contain food stores and rubbish. The eggs are kept in a warm place, and if the nest is under a flat rock which is warmed by the heat of the sun, the eggs are often moved right up under the rock to give them maximum warmth. If you remove the rock, exposing the eggs, the ants hurry them back into a warmer part of the nest.

Army ants

One of the most spectacular ant colonies is that of the army ants, whose activities have earned them many alternative names, such as legionary ants, foraging ants, soldier ants, visiting ants and driver ants. These ants are nomads, who make a base for a few weeks at a time and then move on. They are carnivores and will eat any animal in their path. If there is a house standing in their way, they will go through it like a tornado. If it happens to be your house move out, taking your pets with you, until the army has moved on! But you will have one advantage; the ants will clear the house of every kind of vermin, insects, and other unwel-

238

come intruders who may be in residence.

When the ants decide to camp for the night they make what is called a bivouac, generally in some sheltered spot such as a hollow tree or beneath a branch that has fallen on the ground. The queen, any eggs and larvae, and perhaps some males and immature queens form the heart of the bivouac, around which are layer upon layer of workers, linked together in vertical chains and nets by gripping each other with their claws, and forming a solid 'ball' up to three feet across.

Next morning when the sun is well up, many of the ants leave the bivouac and fan out across the floor of the forest where they live, in search of prey. Every creature that can get out of the way does so, either by burrowing into the ground or flying or climbing out of reach. Anything else is doomed. Gradually a column is formed and the bulk of the ant army marches along one track in search of its food. To maintain the line of march the ants lay down a pheromone or chemical trail, and this is kept renewed as long as the route is in

239

240

At this time the abdomen of the queen enlarges enormously as the ovaries develop and force apart the body plates which come to be separated by large areas of membrane (241). During a few days the queen lays 100,000 eggs or more which are collected and tended by the workers (240). After the egg-laying phase the queen's abdomen returns to normal size again and she is then able to march with her soldiers and workers when the nomadic phase is resumed. Males are produced in the dry season; they are as large as the deflated queen and are hairy and winged (242). Their sole function is to locate and fertilize young queens which are produced at the same time of year.

use. If you watch any line of ants on the march you will notice that they follow the route slavishly – if the trail leads over a twig along the path every ant will go over, even though it is as convenient to go under. That is because the pheromone signposts point in that direction.

Soldier ants often appear to be standing by the side of the route as if directing operations. In fact they are merely on guard duty. The smaller, more active workers are the driving force for the march. Eventually, at some distance from the nest the column breaks up and the ants advance on a broad front several yards wide engulfing all animals that cannot escape.

The ants will form a bridge with their own bodies to cross an awkward place, such as a deep crack in the ground, or even water. With the coming of night the ant army retraces its steps to its bivouac. It will stay in one place for about three weeks; during that time a fresh generation of workers has been laid, hatched, and reared – and, perhaps as important, everything edible within range of the

bivouac set up by the ant army has been eaten.

Eventually the army decides to break camp for good and take to the road. Scouts go ahead to seek out a new home, and a series of one-night stopovers is made. The break-up of the camp happens at dusk, after a normal day's marauding. Suddenly the stream of workers carrying food supplies into the bivouac turns in another direction, and sets off along the trail towards the next selected campsite. Other workers seize the remaining stores and bring them along, together with any eggs and larvae. Finally the queen herself, heavily escorted by a crowd of soldiers, leaves the old camp. By about midnight the ant army has completed its move.

As a rule, the ants do not move while the queen is laying eggs, which she does in bursts of feverish activity. While the army is on the move, the queen does not lay. But a few days after a new bivouac is reached and she has settled down, the queen's body becomes greatly distended, and in the next twenty days or so she produces anything up to 300,000 eggs.

New colonies are formed in the dry season of the year, when the queen produces a number of eggs which give rise to young queens and males. When the new queens hatch, the ant army divides into two factions, one loyal to the old queen, the other clustering around the new ones. Finally, when the males are hatched, the colony breaks up and sets off along two trails towards the next bivouacs. The old queen and her adherents form one party, and the new queens and their supporters form the other. But only one of the young queens is allowed to reach the new bivouac with the daughter colony. The others are held back by workers, and eventually abandoned to die.

On rare occasions the old queen herself is abandoned, and the two groups are each led by a new young queen. This presumably happens when the old queen is reaching the end of her useful life.

The life-style just described is that of most of the dozen or so species that form the genus *Eciton*. But there are more than 200 other species of army ants of varying kinds, and their habits differ considerably. In Africa, driver ants of the genera *Anomma* and *Dorylus* emigrate on a different cycle. *Anomma* queens lay their eggs continuously, and the periods between emigrations may be up to three months. Not surprisingly, an *Anomma* bivouac is a much more permanent affair than that of an *Eciton* army. It has a maze of underground galleries and chambers which make it much more like that of a non-migratory species.

Leaf-cutter ants

Of the many other species of ants, perhaps the most interesting kinds are the farmers, which grow crops for food or raise other insects for their secretions, rather as men keep cows, and those which make slaves of other species of ants and set them to work.

The crop-raising ants belong to the tribe Attini, and there are about 200 species of them in the New World. They have many popular names, the best-known of which is leaf-cutters, because they cut sections out of leaves and take them back to the nests. Because they walk along with the pieces

241

242

of leaf held upright like sunshades, they are also known as parasol ants. Ants of the genus *Atta*, in particular, are a scourge to farmers in many parts of South America and Central America, because of the damage they do to growing crops.

The *Atta* foragers set out from the underground nest to the nearest source of suitable leaf material. This may be a mango tree, a garden, a field of growing plants, or a grove of orange or lemon trees. The range of the ants' raids may be 100 yards or more. The trail is marked in the usual way by pheromones, which the workers themselves renew as they pass along it. Soldiers, which are much larger than the workers, guard the route.

As the ants arrive at the plant they are going to strip they form working parties which set to work methodically to cut up each leaf. The jaws of *Atta* ants are curved so that they can snip out the D-shaped sections, each about the same length as the ants themselves. As an ant completes the cut it maneuvers the section of leaf into the upright carrying position and marches off down the plant

243

243–52. *Atta*, leaf-cutter ants. Leaf-cutter or parasol ants of the genus *Atta* can be serious pests in the New World tropics where they defoliate many kinds of tree and shrub. This they do to provide a compost on which to cultivate the fungus which is their food. Trails consisting of thousands of ants carrying leaf fragments back to the nest are usually found at night (243) although the same nest may at times switch to daytime collecting. The portions of leaf are carried vertically (244) after being cut with the asymmetrical jaws, which operate like a tailor's scissors (245).

Around the underground nest, main trails 4–5 inches wide radiate into the surrounding forest and the soil is beaten flat by the passage of countless tiny feet night after night (246). Leaf-cutters collect systematically; they concentrate their efforts on a particular area each night and may travel several hundred yards from the nest. Each moderate-to-large worker cuts a disc of foliage and carefully positions it between its jaws (247).

stem to the ground with it, and back to the nest. If the piece is dropped another ant will pick it up at ground level and take it away.

The ants are thorough: they destroy each leaf before moving on to the next one, and strip the whole plant completely, even removing flowers.

Once the leaf fragments arrive at the nest they are handed over to other workers, who prepare them for the garden. Each leaf is licked over, and cut into smaller pieces four to eight hundredths of an inch across. Its edges are chewed to speed the process of decay, and the ants then set the tiny leaf sections into the layer of rotting leaf mold which forms the vegetable plot. On this the ants grow a fungus, which is exclusive to ants' nests and is a highly cultivated plant.

The fungus produces a series of tiny heads or swellings, known as conidia, and it is on these that the ants feed. The fungus is never allowed to reach the fruiting stage. Extra small worker-ants tend the gardens, removing and eating any unwanted spores that have been accidentally brought in on the leaf cuttings. Some species of ants manure their gardens, using their own feces for the purpose and thus ensuring a better crop. Substances in the manure also seem to inhibit the growth of unwanted strains of fungi.

244

245

When *Atta* ants form a new colony, they take the fungus with them. *Atta* colonies are founded by a single queen, who makes a mating flight and then sets up on her own in a little nest which she digs into the soil. Before setting off on her mating flight the queen stuffs a little wad of fungus into a cavity near her gullet. When she has excavated her nesting chamber she regurgitates the wad of fungus, which rapidly grows. The queen tends the garden until the first workers have hatched and matured sufficiently to take over the work. The fungus is used not only as food for the workers, but is also fed to the growing larvae.

Other ants

A great many species of ants are seed-gatherers, like primitive man before he learned to grow crops. These go by the general name of harvester ants.

246

247

The harvesters live in the desert or semi-desert regions of the world. They take seeds back to their nests and store them in granary cells for consumption when food is in short supply.

The pastoral ants seek out a secretion known as honeydew. This sweet secretion is produced by many of the insects of the suborder Homoptera – aphids, scale insects, plant lice, and others – and also by the caterpillars of some butterflies. These insects all feed on sap, and the honeydew is the by-product of their feeding. A great many species of ants collect this scattered honeydew, but some, including many in the genus *Formica*, actually tend the aphids. An ant will walk up to an aphid which is gorged with honeydew and gently caress its body with her antennae. The aphid at once voids a droplet of honeydew, which the ant consumes. When it is gorged it returns to the nest.

An aphid that is continually milked in this way has a higher output of honeydew than one which is untended, so the ants' attentions are not without their effect. In addition, the presence of the ants

The fragment is then carried down the shrub or tree (248), which may be 60 or more feet high, to join the trail of other ants hurrying home. Soldiers, distinguished by their larger size and huge heads, guard the trail at intervals (249). Very small individuals also accompany the foragers but do not cut leaves; it is thought that their function may be to protect their larger brethren from attack by parasitic flies and also to collect water. The small individuals frequently ride back on leaves carried by their big sisters. One such hitch-hiker is seen about to be carried into one of the several nest entrances (250). A large nest may cover a quarter of an acre and contain fungus gardens down to a depth of several feet. The queen lives in one of the deeper cells; she is huge by comparison with the workers who tend her (251). Apart from collecting foliage the workers prepare the compost and look after the fungus which feeds the colony (252).

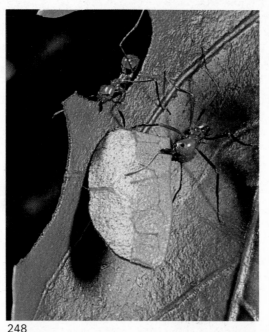

248

249

250

acts as a protection for the aphid herd; intruders are driven off by the ants with sprays of formic acid, and in cases of extreme danger the ants are known to pick up the aphids and carry them to safety. The protection provided by the ants results in a growth of the aphid population.

Some species of ants go further in their care for the aphid herds. Many ants in the genus *Cremato-gaster* go so far as to build shelters on the plant stems to protect the aphids as they feed. These shelters may be made of cemented earth, but a paper-like substance, similar to the paper used by wasps in their nests is more generally used.

Some ants move their cattle from one plant to another, usually to give them better pasturage. In North America, the corn-root aphid, *Aphis maid-iradicus*, is even more closely looked after by ants of the species *Lasius americana*. As winter approaches the ants carry aphid eggs down into the nests, where they tend them through the cold-weather period. With the return of spring the ants carry the freshly-hatched young aphids out and set them grazing on nearby grasses, moving them to the young corn plants as these grow.

The problem of storing honeydew for future use has been overcome by some species of ants which have developed a special sub-caste of workers known as repletes. Repletes are capable of storing large quantities of honeydew in their crops, and develop huge, greatly distended bodies, thus serving as living store-rooms. When their stores are needed they regurgitate the honeydew. Repletes are found among ants in North America, southern Africa, and Australia.

Aphids are not the only house-guests tolerated or encouraged by ants. Insects that live in ants' nests are known as myrmecophiles, literally 'ant-lovers,' and there are many kinds. One group functions as scavengers, and includes many rove-beetles of the family Staphylinidae. These beetles prey on dead or sick ants, and are not encouraged by the ants themselves in any way: in fact they have to keep well clear of the ants. A much larger group consists of various insects which are toler-

251

252

ated by the ants and live in the nests for protection. They include the larvae of various beetles and flies, and some of the beetles are mimics of their hosts. Finally, there are a number of insects, mostly beetles of various kinds, which the ants actively encourage, feeding, grooming, and even rearing them. As with the aphids, ants do all this in return for a substance secreted by the guests.

Sometimes ants of more than one species are found sharing the same nest. But most sharing of this kind is a form of parasitism, with one species relying on the other for shelter. The queens of the wood ant species *Formica rufa*, for example, hardly ever seem to found a new colony by excavating a nest chamber of their own. As a rule a queen of this species enters the nest of another species and uses part of it to rear her first brood. Many queens are intercepted and killed by workers of the invaded nests, but enough survive to ensure that *Formica rufa* is a fairly common species. Their nests generally contain more than one queen.

In one species, *Formica exsecta*, the queen may

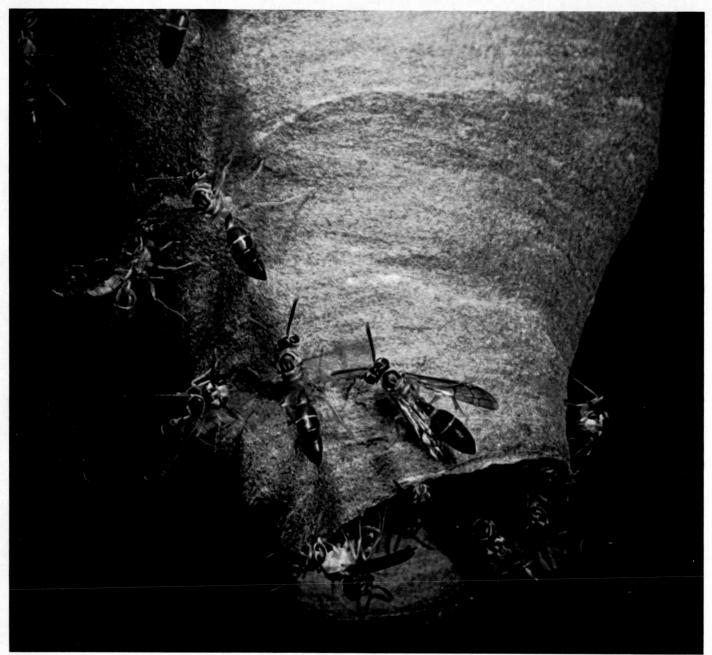

253

253. The nest of *Stelo-polybia pallens* is shaped like an inverted flask with the entrance at the bottom. When disturbed the wasps cluster over the outside of the nest and make a loud rustling noise which sounds extremely ominous. Sufficient, at least, to make this photographer decide to move on quickly!

254. *Vespa vulgaris*, like other social wasps, makes its nest of chewed wood, known as 'wasp paper.' The different colors indicate the various sources from which the wood has been collected. Although generally regarded as a nuisance because of the damage they do to fruit, wasps are beneficial in destroying large numbers of caterpillars.

in fact take over the colony completely. A young, newly mated queen of this species will hang around outside another nest, and pretend to be dead. Workers of the unwitting host nest carry her inside, where she hides, often in the cell of the host ants' queen. Within a few days she contrives to kill the host queen, and from then on it is her eggs which the workers look after. Soon the workers of the host colony have died off, and the colony is entirely monopolized by the offspring of the intruder. The queen overcomes the problem of having the wrong smell by waiting around for a few days until she too has absorbed the family scent, and is accepted by the hosts.

Some species of ants have become notorious for actually making slaves. One of the best-known is the robber ant, *Formica sanguinea*. A raiding party of robber ants makes its way to the nest of another species of ant, which will generally be of the same genus, such as *Formica fusca*, the Negro ant. There they capture as many pupae as possible and carry them back to their own nest, only fight-

254

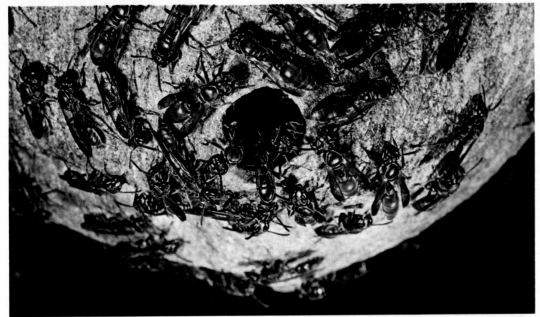

255

256

255. When members of OSF arrived to stay at the Simla Research Station in Trinidad a nest of grapefruit size belonging to the wasp *Polybia rejecta* was hanging above the front door. It soon became apparent that the wasps were not prepared to share the entrance with humans -- the wasps won! -- and OSF was obliged to use the rear entrance. Three months later the nest had been enlarged to the size of a football and contained several thousand wasps. Then, one afternoon, a foraging party of army ants found the nest. The wasps at once moved out while the ants removed all the brood over a period of four hours. The wasps hung up in a bunch on the foliage of a nearby tree, but they did not reoccupy the empty nest after the ants had gone and OSF was at last able to use the front door!

256. *Apoica pallida* is unusual in being nocturnal. During the daytime the wasps hang from the comb; at night they are active and, since they are attracted to light, and have a powerful sting, they can make night photography in Trinidad an uncomfortable experience!

ing and killing the Negro ant workers if they venture to offer battle. The robber ants eat a proportion of the captured larvae, and allow the rest to hatch out. The Negro ant workers then act as slaves for the robber ants, though they otherwise appear to enjoy equal rights in the nest. The warrior ants of the genus *Polyergus*, the amazon ants, rely entirely on slaves for running their nests. Their mandibles are so shaped that they make first-class weapons, but are useless as tools. Without slaves, the amazon ants would literally starve to death, and would be unable to look after their eggs or their larvae. In between raids they spend their time lounging about the nest, demanding food from the slaves or grooming themselves.

Termites

The other group of social insects, whose organization outstrips even that of the ants, is that of the termites, the wrongly-termed white ants mostly found in tropical or semi-tropical zones. Termites may look like ants superficially, but in terms of insect development they are much more primitive, and their closest relatives are the cockroaches. Termites form their own order, the Isoptera.

An interesting aspect of the termites is that, although they have a very different ancestry and evolution from that of the ants, bees and wasps, they have evolved quite independently a very similar social structure. However, having formed a social pattern, they appear to have stayed with it, and do not have the wide variety of life styles that we find among the ants. The 2,000 or so species vary greatly in size, from the huge *Macrotermes bellicosus* of Africa, which is up to five inches in length, to the tiny species in the genus *Afrosubulitermes*, about twelve hundredths of an inch long.

Like the social insects of the Hymenoptera, termites have a caste system. At the head of it is the queen, who is very much larger than other kinds of termites. But here is the first and biggest difference between the termites and the ants. The queen has a consort, the king, who is smaller than his spouse. He mates with her at the founding of

257

257–9. *Nasutitermes ephratae*. The tree nest of this termite is a familiar sight in the high forest of Trinidad (257). In section the nest is seen to consist of a multitude of small interconnected chambers (258). The building material is a mixture of chewed wood, saliva and the termites' own faeces. The queen, which has a greatly distended abdomen, occupies a large cell somewhere near the center of the nest (259). Locating the queen cell entails carefully sectioning the nest, slice by slice, a procedure that may take several hours.

Some have sharp mandibles that snap together and can inflict a nasty bite; some can flick one mandible against another, to give an opponent a powerful blow; some produce a corrosive chemical spray, which turns glue-like on exposure to air, trapping and corroding enemies, and some have no special weapons but use their large heads to block the galleries of the nest against intruders.

The foundation of a new termite colony starts at the beginning of the rainy season when the workers make breaches in the walls of the nest and permit a certain number of males and females of the royal caste, the reproductives, to escape and take to the air. This is not a mating flight, but serves to disperse the termites. When the flight is over the termites shed their wings, and the males seek out the females in order to pair off. The newly engaged pair do not mate until they have found a suitable home. Most termites live in soil or damp wood, and merely have to locate a suitable crevice, but some make their homes in sound wood, and must excavate a cell in it in order to set up home. Then they mate.

The first eggs are cared for by both parents, and take several weeks to develop and hatch. Unlike the Hymenoptera, the termites do not go through a complete metamorphosis. What hatches from the egg is a nymph, basically a miniature version of the adult, although sexually immature. The nymphs go through up to ten stages, molting between each. During the molt the nymph goes through a resting period which may last for several days. Nymphs of the worker caste begin work after the first molt, and continue for the rest of their lives.

Termites generally are long lived. As far as we can tell some of the higher termite species have queens and kings which live for anything from 15 to 50 years, and it is thought some queens can live for up to a century. The royal pair mate at regular intervals throughout their lives, so the queens do not store vast quantities of sperms, like ant and bee queens. Workers and soldiers have shorter lives, but these may survive for about four years.

The life span of a termite colony may be anything from a dozen years to a century, depending on the species. In some species, such as *Nasutitermes triodiae* of Australia, the life of the colony depends on the life of the royal pair. Once the queen dies there are no more eggs, and the colony slowly perishes. One well-established *Nasutitermes* nest was examined in 1872 and again 63 years later, and was still flourishing.

The size of termite colonies varies with the species. The more primitive types have populations of only a few hundreds of thousands; but many colonies run to a million or more.

The diet of termites is varied. The majority of the species eat wood in one form or another; others eat grass and plant debris, and a few species have the same life-style as leaf-cutter ants, making and tending fungus gardens. The main constituent of wood is cellulose, and this the termites are unable to digest. However, their intestines are home for a host of bacteria and protozoans – one-celled animals – which can digest wood cellulose; in fact, as two American professors, Carl Duncan and Gayle Pickwell, once happily phrased it, 'the

the colony, and then spends the rest of his long life with her. The majority of the termites in a nest are wingless workers, but these may be of either sex, though neither is capable of mating or reproducing. In a well-developed nest there are also a large number of soldiers, whose duties appear to be purely defensive.

There are many variations among the workers and soldiers, and these variations depend on the species. In the most highly developed termites, those forming the family Termitidae, there are large and small workers. In the larger species, the males are larger than the females, and it is the males which forage outside the nest, while the females stay at home and do the housework. In smaller species males and females may be about the same size, or the females may even be larger than the males.

Soldiers exist in up to three forms: major, intermediate and minor. The role of soldier termites seems to be the same in all species, but the weapons with which they are equipped vary.

258

259

intestine of a termite is a combination botanical garden and zoological park.'

To obtain their food the termites may make foraging expeditions, but generally they prefer to remain under cover and tunnel their way to dinner. In addition to any fallen timber that may be in contact with the soil in which they live, the termites will attack living trees and of course any man-made timber structures. Some chew their way through the lead covering of underground cables. A number of species make covered ways on the surface of the ground to reach their goal, passing over rock and stone and even up over brick foundations to attack timber on buildings.

The depredations of termites on timber are not always detected at once, because they hollow out the wood and leave the surface intact. At the slightest blow the timber will crumble to dust.

Primitive termites make their homes in the wood on which they feed, constructing a series of galleries and raising there small colonies. But the most spectacular termite homes are the elaborate

260–2 *Zootermopsis angusticollis*. New termite colonies are founded by the very few winged males and females that survive the hazards of swarming from the nest where they were reared and which are also fortunate enough to meet when they descend to earth. (260) shows a lucky pair of *Zootermopsis angusticollis* which have shed their now redundant wings and have excavated a home in damp wood, usually a fallen log. The soldier caste in this species has large jaws (261) for the defense of the colony. When the colony has become well established with plenty of workers, nymphs of a new reproductive generation are produced. These are easily distinguished by the wing pads (262); workers and soldiers are wingless.

263. *Leptotyphlops albifrons* is only 6 inches long when full grown and can claim to be the smallest snake in the world. It is adapted to worming its way through the galleries in nests of termites, e.g. *Nasutitermes* spp. where it feeds on the inmates.

260

261

structures known as termitaria, which are made particularly by species in Africa and Australia, and in parts of Central and South America.

A termitarium begins as a series of galleries and chambers excavated in the ground, centered on the royal cell where the queen and king live. It is a cell in more ways than one, for the royal couple are larger than their attendant workers, and the queen in particular grows to an enormous size. It used to be thought that since the galleries leading from the royal apartment are only big enough for the workers, the royal pair are literally imprisoned for life. But this is not in fact true; the swollen body of the queen can 'flow' through small openings and she will move laboriously to another part of the nest if the chamber is threatened.

The earth that is excavated is used to form further galleries and chambers above ground. The soil is cemented together with saliva, and sets to a rock-like consistency, which is hard to break even with a pick-axe. Only the professional termite-

eaters such as the aardvark of southern Africa seem able to smash their way in with ease. Termitaria reach considerable heights above ground, particularly in Australia. There, the species *Nasutitermes triodiae* constructs steeple-like nests which are many feet high. Some of eighteen feet high, with a diameter of ninety feet at the base, have been recorded. The African species *Macrotermes bellicosus* builds even taller structures – some have measured more than twenty-seven feet – but with bases only about nine feet across.

Investigations of the termitaria of *Macrotermes natalensis* in the Ivory Coast show that the insects design their nest to keep a constant temperature of 86°, no matter what the external temperature is. The outer walls are hard as concrete and about eighteen inches thick. On the outside are a number of vertical ribs which work as the fins of a radiator. Air passages in these ribs lead up to a roof-level chamber where hot, stale air from the nest collects. It passes down through the air vents in the ribs, where it not only cools off but also filters

262

263

out through thousands of very tiny holes. These serve the same function as a lung, admitting fresh oxygen and discharging carbon dioxide. The cooler air falls down into another large chamber underground, from where it circulates upwards through the termitarium's passages and cells.

Although this system is largely automatic in operation, some termite workers are always busy closing up or enlarging air vents according to the outside temperature, in order to maintain an exact internal level of heat.

Incidentally, these structures are erected at surprising speed. Mounds high enough to be a menace to aircraft have been constructed on airfields in the tropics literally overnight.

Termites living in places such as the Amazon River valley of South America where flooding is frequent make their nests not only above ground but actually in trees. The nests are made of wood pulp, a substance called carton by zoologists. Some nests are up to one yard across; others consist of carton tubes radiating along branches.

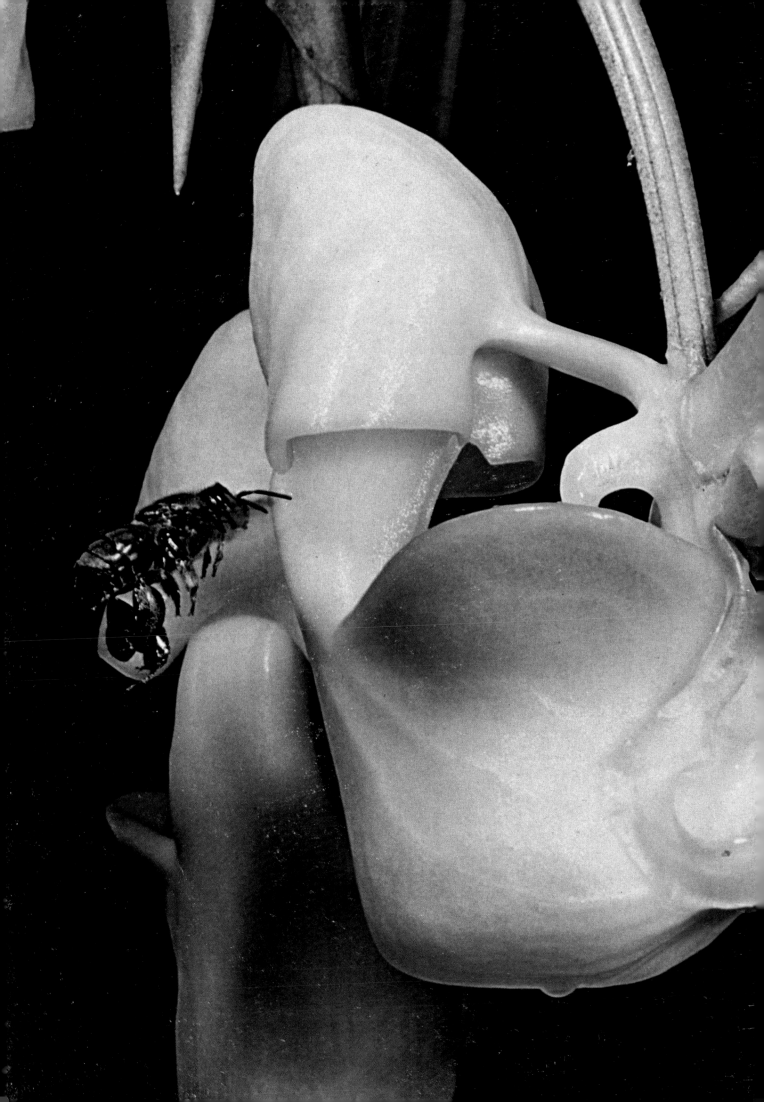

Chapter 7

Insects and their Environment

The hidden world of insects is part of a much larger world: that shared by all other living creatures. As a class, insects are the most successful and widely spread of all land animals. They cannot thrive in the very coldest parts of the polar regions, nor on the windy and snow-swept peaks of the highest mountains. But they are found everywhere else in burning deserts, raging streams, deep in caves, and inside both plants and other animals.

In all these situations insects have an important part to play, for they form an essential part of many food chains, as described on page 55. In proportion to their size they exert a fantastic influence on all plants and animals, including man. Without them many of our plants would cease to multiply, while others would grow unchecked.

Insects vary in type not only according to the climatic conditions of the regions in which they live, but also in the ecological zones – the forests, plains, deserts, tundra, snow and ice. Generally speaking, insects in a particular zone, such as a forest, tend to be of similar types, no matter in what part of the world the forest is located. Certain geographical regions also have their own characteristic insect populations. In this respect it is remarkable that Australia, which has a unique population of marsupial mammals, shares its insect types with the islands and mainland of south-eastern Asia. Africa, on the contrary, has mammals common to other parts of the world but many of the species of insects found there are unique.

Other insects flourish only in certain climatic conditions. For example, bumblebees live in the temperate regions of the northern hemisphere and are rarely found in the tropics. Termites flourish mostly in the tropics, and only a few are found in the more northerly regions of Europe, Asia, and North America. It is notable, too, that the largest insects all come from tropical lands. These include the hercules emperor moth, *Coscinoscera hercules*, of New Guinea and northern Australia, which has a wingspan of up to ten inches; the giant birdwing butterfly, *Troides victoriae*, which has an even bigger wingspan and lives in the Solomon Islands; and a four-inch bush cricket, *Pseudophyllanax imperialis*, which lives in another Pacific island, New Caledonia. South and Central America have more than their fair share of giant

insects, including the largest fly, the robber-fly *Mydas heros*; the largest wasp, *Pepsis frivaldskii*; and such generally large insects as the *Morpho* butterflies, which seem to glide rather than fly through the air on their huge, brilliantly blue-colored wings.

Population densities

Generally speaking, insect populations remain remarkably steady, if studied over a long period of time. But they may fluctuate wildly from year to year, and in some years great population explosions occur in certain localities. It is well known that the lemming, a close relative of the vole, which lives in Scandinavia, suddenly increases in numbers every three or four years – so much so that mass emigration becomes necessary. The years in which the lemmings increase also tend to produce butterfly epidemics, and forests are defoliated by the hungry caterpillars.

A familiar example of insect population explosions is provided by the locusts (Acrididae). From time to time several species in this family multiply enormously, and migrate in huge, destructive swarms, devouring all the crops in those regions where they happen to settle for any length of time.

Within a given environment, too many insects of one kind place too great a strain on the food supply. The insects die from starvation or become victims of disease, perhaps brought about by undernourishment and overcrowding. Viruses and bacteria multiply readily in such conditions, and so do parasites. Then the balance of nature, after seesawing wildly, returns to equilibrium once more.

The effect of insects on plant life at times of population explosion can be calamitous. But in normal times insects are beneficial to plant life, and indeed insects and plants have evolved together. Flowers have evolved colors and scents that are attractive to insects, while insects have developed senses that can detect flowers that they need as food.

Pollination of flowers

Like the majority of insects, all but a very few flowers reproduce sexually. A typical flower has both male and female organs within it. The pistils contain the ovules, or egg-cases, while the stamens

264. Orchids of the genus *Coryanthes* have the most complicated pollination mechanism known in the plant kingdom. The pollinating agent is the male of a beautiful green metallic euglossine bee.

265

265. Larvae of beetles of the
family Dermestidae feed on
fur, hides and felt as well as
bacon and cheese, and are
extremely destructive. Some
species have become almost
cosmopolitan.

266. Certain species of
termite excavate their
galleries in dry timber,
although the insects usually
require access to moisture.
The excavations never
penetrate to the outside and
the first sign of the termites'
presence may be the collapse
of the structure.

266

bear the pollen which is the fertile male element.
For the flower to develop a seed or seeds, the
pollen must be brought into contact with the
ovules. Some flowers are self-pollinating, and
need no outside help. But many rely on the visits
of insects, attracted to the flower either by pollen,
which many insects use for food, or by nectar, a
sweet fluid secreted by specialized parts of the
flower. A bee burrowing deep into a blossom to
reach the nectar becomes covered by pollen,
which brushes off and fertilizes the female part of
the flower. Many plants – marrows and cucum-
bers, for example – have separate male and female
flowers, and depend completely on the inter-
vention of outside agencies such as insects for
fertilization.

Of course, not all insects play a part in pollination. Bees are probably the most important of
the pollinating insects, and butterflies, moths, and
flies also help in the process. Most beetles are
plant destroyers rather than pollinators, but some,
for example, certain tropical chafer beetles, pol-

linate flowers while eating them. Many insects and
flowers are specially adapted to each other, just
as many parasites can survive only on one type
of host. The yucca flowers of North America are
fertilized only by the yucca moths of the genus
Pronuba, which lay their eggs in the ovaries of the
yucca flowers, and in the course of doing so transfer pollen from one flower to another. Some
flowers, such as soapwort *Saponaria officinalis* are
so constructed that only an insect with a very
long proboscis such as the hummingbird hawk
moth, *Macroglossum stellatarum*, can reach the
nectar.

Insects' value to mankind

Insects react with man just as they do with
every other form of life on the land surface of the
earth. People tend to regard insects as either
beneficial or pests, but one and the same insect
can be both according to how you look at its life
and work. For example, the wasp that stings you is
decidedly a pest – but it may have been scaveng-
ing for rotten fruit or destroying harmful caterpillars in your garden.

Insects, besides usefully pollinating plants, provide food in many parts of the world. But even
those people who do not eat the insects themselves eat their products. Besides honey, popular
in all parts of the world, there is manna, the
miraculous food on which the Children of Israel
fed in the wilderness. This manna is a sweet-
tasting secretion exuded by tamarisk trees in
Sinai when they are pierced by scale insects.
Scale insects also provide two dyestuffs, cochineal
and the crimson *kermes* of ancient Greece. Some
insects are used in medicine, mostly by people in
the developing countries; though even as recently as World War I the maggots of certain flies
were used by some medical experimenters to help
clean infected wounds.

Insect secretions of importance include waxes
of various kinds, particularly beeswax, and shellac,
a waxy, resinous compound produced by the lac
insect, *Laccifer lacca*, which is a species of scale insect. Each insect exudes only a minute amount of
lac, the basic substance of shellac – and nearly
200,000 insects may be needed to produce two
pounds of the substance. The abundance of
shellac shows the enormous numbers of insects
that exist. Incidentally, lac comes from the Hindu
word lakh, meaning 100,000.

It is remarkable that of all the million or more
species of insects, only two have ever been truly
domesticated and bred by man for his own purposes. They are the honey bee, *Apis mellifera* and
the silkworm moth, *Bombyx mori*.

Pests and disease-carriers

When it comes to the question of insect pests,
the picture is not so clear. Broadly speaking, an
insect pest is one which eats something man
requires for his own use, whether it be the crops
in the fields, the clothes in the wardrobe, or even
the timbers of his house and furniture. But these
insects are only pests insofar as they compete
with man; of themselves they may well be highly
beneficial. For example, the various wood-boring
beetles greatly speed up the process of decay in

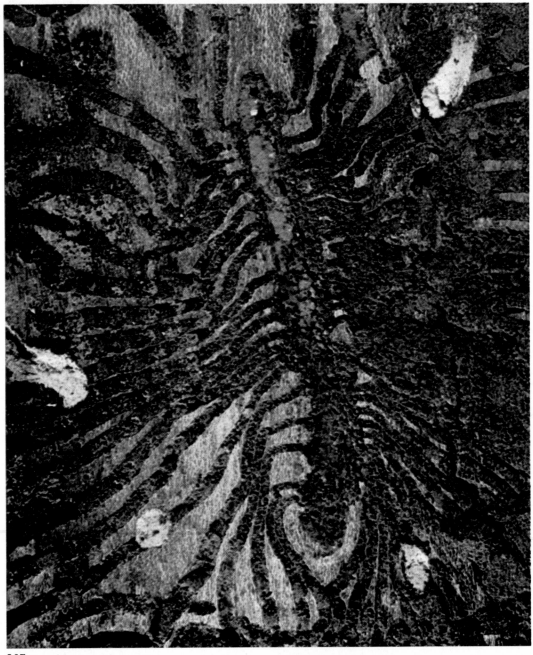

267

268

267. The bark beetle, *Scolytus scolytus*, is one of the main vectors of the fungus which causes Dutch elm disease. The mother beetle lays her eggs in a central gallery beneath the bark of a dead elm tree and the larvae tunnel outwards more or less radially into the surrounding bark.

268. Bees are among the most important pollinators of flowers. This bee is carrying an immense load of pollen as it leaves an Easter lily.

fallen trees, and without them forests would choke with the piled-up timber. In tropical countries which lack modern sanitation the vast army of dung-rolling beetles are of inestimable benefit.

It is convenient to group insect pests into four categories: those which damage crops, those which damage or destroy other materials, those which cause harm to animals, and those which are dangerous to man.

Any crop cultivated by man is necessarily a deliberate attempt to change the balance of nature by over-producing one type of vegetation. Not surprisingly, every cultivated plant has its own insect pests. Man himself contributes to the spread of these pests by moving grain and fruit from one part of the world to another, and unwittingly moving the insects with them. Often an insect that is thus forcefully transplanted to a new environment flourishes even better there than in its natural habitat, because the predators and other checks on its rapid development are not so numerous in the new setting.

268

269. Many aphids are
tended by ants which feed
on the sweet excreta, known
as honeydew, which aphids
produce in large quantity.
The ants give the aphids
protection by repelling other
predatory insects.

269

A notorious example of an insect pest that was spread by man is the plant louse *Viteus vitifolii*, formerly *V. Phylloxera*. This species originated in North America and was accidentally introduced into Europe, where in 1863 it killed off enormous quantities of vines, practically bringing the French wine industry to a standstill and completely stopping wine production in Madeira and the Canary Islands. More recently another American pest, the Colorado beetle, *Leptinotarsa decemlineata*, was also introduced into Europe, where it has ravaged potato crops. This transfer of insect pests across the Atlantic Ocean is a two-way traffic: the European cornborer, *Pyrausta nubialis*, is a serious threat to American corn crops, while the cabbage butterfly, *Pieris rapae*, has spread from Europe to prey on the green vegetable crops grown in North America, Australia and New Zealand.

Specialist pests of various crops include many weevils, such as the boll weevil, *Anthonomus grandis*, which devours cotton; the banana weevil,

Cosmopolites sordidus, which attacks bananas; and the pea and bean weevils of the family Bruchidae, which prey on the plants whose names they bear. The larvae of moths attack a wide range of plants, including apples, stone fruit, cotton plants, maize, millet, rice and sorghum. Various flies and their maggots attack fruit trees and bushes as well as other plants.

In addition to the damage they do to crops by eating them, insects can also act as carriers of disease-producing organisms – viruses, bacteria, and fungi. Dutch elm disease, which kills elm trees and is so-named because it was first identified in the Netherlands, is caused by a fungus, *Ceratocystis ulmi*. The spread of the fungus has been aided by various bark beetles in the subfamily Scolytinae. Logs carrying not only the fungus but also larvae of the European elm bark beetle, *Scolytus scolytus*, were exported from Europe to North America. The beetles transmitted the fungus, and also passed it on to the native American bark beetle, *Hylurgopinus rufipes*.

270

Most virus diseases of plants are transmitted by insects, particularly aphids and leafhoppers.

Beetles and moths take the biggest toll of other materials, mostly stored food and timber. As an order, beetles have catholic tastes, and it is mostly their larvae which do the damage.

Insects which attack animals include the warble flies, whose activities are described on page 59, biting and sucking lice, and fleas. Many of them also transmit disease. The various flies which infect open wounds with their maggots, such as blowflies and screw-worm flies, probably cause the most damage and the greatest loss of life.

Man himself is attacked by a comparatively limited number of insects, and few of these – wasps, mosquitoes and lice, for example, do more than cause inconvenience by biting or stinging. But many of the most serious diseases are transmitted by insects, some of them with the aid of other animals. The most notorious is plague; the Black Death of the fourteenth century killed a quarter of the population of Europe, and the Great Plague which ravaged London in 1664–5, spread by the rat flea, killed one person in six.

Malaria is caused by a single-celled organism known as *Plasmodium*, and is carried by mosquitoes of the genus *Anopheles*. Control of the disease is generally achieved by eliminating the mosquitoes.

Other serious diseases transmitted by insects include typhoid, carried by houseflies and cockroaches; cholera, carried by the same insects; dysentery, also carried by houseflies; and yellow fever, transmitted by mosquitoes. Sleeping sickness is transmitted by tsetse flies (Glossina). Trypanosomiasis, to give the disease its medical name, affects many mammals besides man, and over large areas of tropical Africa the presence of the disease and its carriers prevents the rearing of cattle.

Insect control

In the never-ending fight to preserve his own health and his food supplies, man has resorted

270. This species of *Opsiphanes* comes from Trinidad. Butterflies imbibe liquid food, usually nectar, through a long proboscis which is coiled up out of the way when not in use.

271. The bed bug *Cimex lectularius* is an inhabitant of houses, living in cracks and crevices. Bed bugs are only found on man when visiting to feed. Although they are a nuisance they do not transmit diseases.

272 *Rhodnius prolixus* is a South American assassin bug (Reduviidae) much used in physiological research. Its bite is quite painless but it transmits chagas disease, which is caused by a protozoan parasite (*Trypanosoma*) closely related to the species that causes sleeping sickness in Africa

273. In this close-up view of *Rhodnius* the characteristic hemipteran mouthparts can be seen inserted into human skin while taking a blood meal.

271

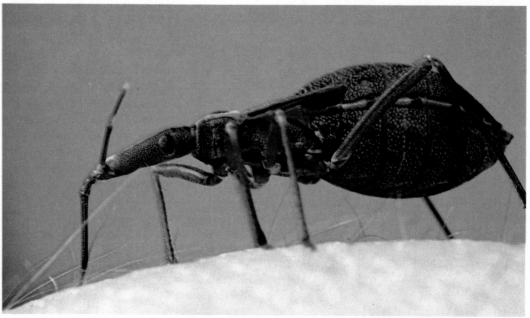

272

273

to a great number of different ways of controlling insects.

However, the greatest stride forward – or so it seemed at the time – was produced by the development of the insecticide DDT in the 1940s. This powerful killing agent's full name is *dichloro-diphenyl-trichloroethane*. Its early victories were spectacular: in 1944 an epidemic of typhus fever in Naples was stopped by using DDT powder to kill body lice, which carried the disease. Its use was rapidly extended to all kinds of insect pests, and it helped to curb malaria in many places by killing the mosquitoes.

But DDT also produced several unexpected and undesirable results. First of all, it killed not only the insect pests but also the valuable insects with which it came into contact. Then, over the years, strains of insects which were proof against DDT gradually evolved. And finally it was found that other forms of animal life which eat insects were being poisoned by DDT, and that streams, rivers, and even the Great Lakes of North America were

274

being polluted by the chemical. The widespread use of DDT in the United States was severely curbed by law during the early 1970s. Other pesticides tried as alternatives, such as endrin, were found to be equally harmful. Endrin kills birds and fish and harms other animals.

A more desirable way of curbing pests is by the use of biological control, which is less likely to have unwanted side-effects. Biological control has usually entailed introducing the natural enemies of an insect pest and in the past these have mostly been insect parasites or predators. Much current research, however, is being devoted to the use of viruses in the perpetual war against those insects which prey on valuable crops.

Another application of biological control has involved breeding large numbers of insects in laboratories, and sterilizing the males by means of ionizing radiation. The males are then released in infected areas in numbers much greater than the natural population. A high proportion of the wild females mate with the sterile males, and as a

result no offspring are produced by their union.

One of the earliest victories over insect pests by this method was won in the south-eastern United States, where it was used successfully against the screw-worm fly, *Callitroga macellaria*. This insect, a relative of the familiar blowfly, lays its eggs on animals and man, and the larvae burrow into the skin.

The predatory nature of some insects can be used to control other insect pests. An early example of the successful use of an insect predator was against the fluted scale insect, *Icerya purchasi*. After it was accidentally introduced into California it rapidly threatened the important citrus plantations. An Australian ladybug, *Rodolia cardinalis*, was imported into California and quickly brought the scale insects under control. This ladybug has been used in other places where scale insects have proved a danger to citrus fruit farms. Unfortunately, indiscriminate use of modern powerful pesticides has tended to kill off the ladybugs while allowing the scale insects to flourish,

274. Horseflies (Tabanidae) have a painful bite but are generally harmless. In Africa, however, they may carry the nematode worm *Loa loa* which is parasitic in man.

275, 276. The tsetse fly *Glossina austeni* lives in the forests of East Africa. Tsetse flies carry the dreaded sleeping sickness which kills both man and his cattle. It is caused by protozoan blood parasites belonging to the genus Trypanosoma.
After feeding (276) the abdomen is inflated with blood. In this specimen the tracheal network is particularly conspicuous.

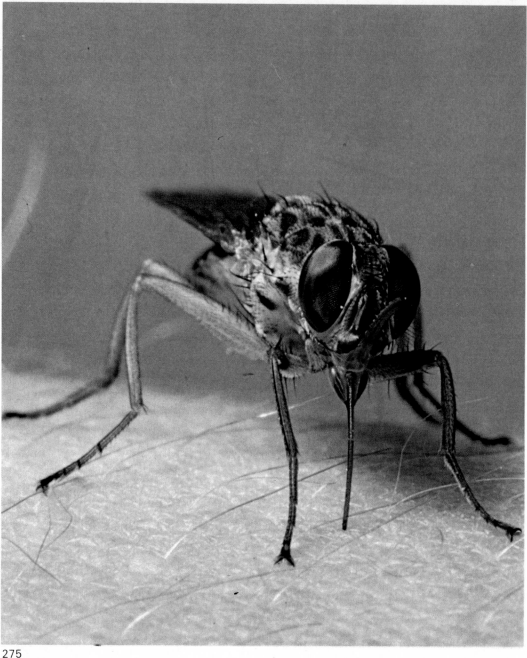

275

and so the problem is once more arising in various parts of the world.

The use of herbivores in this way is not without its dangers. An attempt in New Zealand to control blackberry bushes, which had been imported from Britain and rapidly became rampant as weeds, had to be abandoned because any potential enemies would be likely to attack two of New Zealand's important commercial crops, raspberries and apples.

Sometimes the complications provide an unexpected bonus. An epidemic of European sawflies in eastern Canada was tackled by introducing the sawflies' natural parasites. With the parasites came virus diseases, and these diseases killed off the sawflies even faster than the parasites could have done.

Biological control has two great advantages: if successful, it is usually permanent, and it is cheap. Breeding a few thousand insects in a laboratory and flying them to another part of the world generally costs only a few thousand dollars. Once set to work, the insects require no further expenditure, beyond an occasional inspection to see how they are getting on. Using the large quantities of chemical pesticides needed for control is a matter of much more money, and not only in one down-payment, but over years of repeated applications.

The balance of nature is a very complex subject, and any attempt to interfere with it is likely to lead to trouble. In this balance the insects in their hidden world play a much greater part than most people realize.

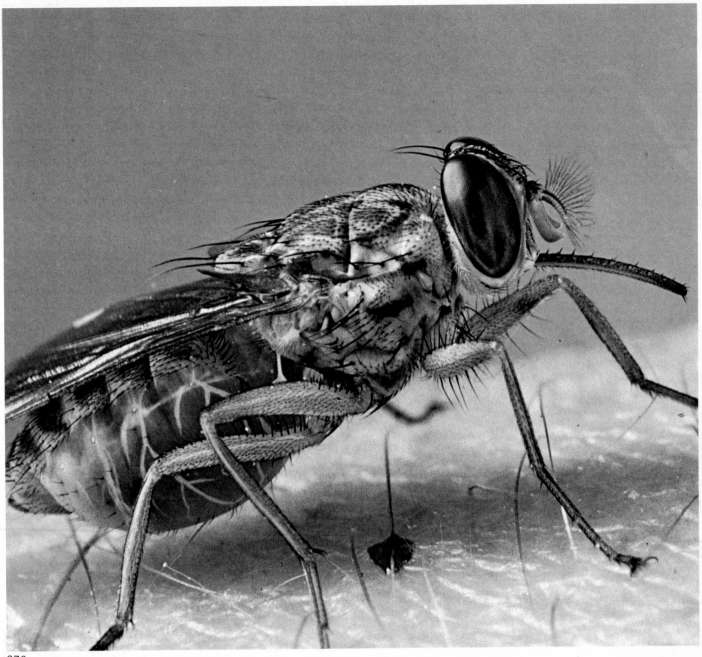

276

277   278

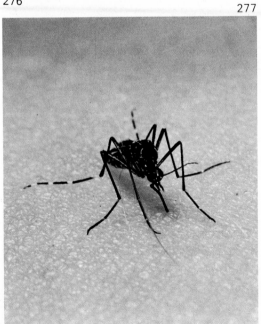

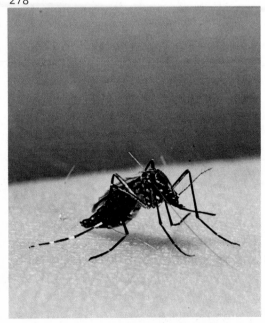

277, 278. Females of the mosquito *Aedes aegypti*, here shown feeding on man, are of great medical importance. They transmit several virus diseases, notably dengue and yellow fevers. Other mosquito species also transmit malaria, as well as filarial worms. After feeding (278) the mosquito body becomes grossly distended with blood.

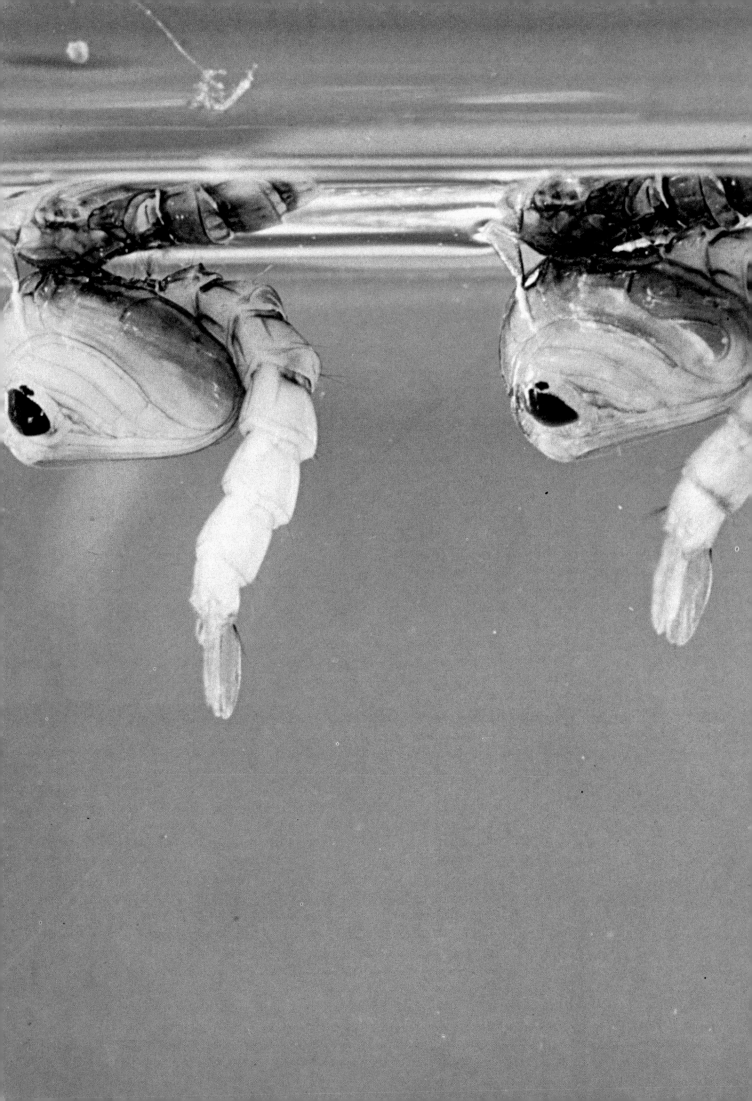

Index

Back endpaper: eye spot on the hind wing of a wild silk moth.

Acknowledgements

We would like to thank the following individuals and institutions for advice, assistance and specimens. Fred D. Bennett, Commonwealth Institute of Biological Control, Trinidad; Professor Jake Kenny and Dr David Stradling, University of the West Indies, Trinidad; Claude Rivers, Unit of Plant Pathology, University of Oxford; Vince Roth, S.W. Research Station, American Museum of Natural History; the staff of the Asa Wright Nature Centre, Trinidad; the Department of Entomology, British Museum; the Hope Department of Entomology, University of Oxford; the Glasshouse Crops Research Institute, Rustington; the London School of Hygiene and Tropical Medicine; the Liverpool School of Tropical Medicine; the Tsetse Research Laboratory, Department of Veterinary Medicine, Bristol. Special thanks are due to David Thompson for the slide series on the honey bee and locust.